Tears in the Wind

Triumph and Tragedy on America's Highest Peak

Larry Semento

Tears in the Wind

Copyright © 2016

ISBN-10:1533558132

ISBN-13:978-1533558138

Lawrence J. Semento

Editor: Michael Sherson

Cover Design: Angie Alaya

Table of Contents

Foreword 1

Author's Introduction.............................4

The Seeds are Planted 8

Climbing Fever.................................... 13

Denali Dreaming.................................19

May 19-Welcome to Alaska.................... 44

May 20-On To Talkeetna 47

May 21-The Ascent Begins.....................55

May 22-The Beauty of the Mountain 75

May 23-Sitting Out a Snowstorm 80

May 24-Fried by the Sun........................ 83

May 25-Denali Turns Deadly................... 86

May 26-Climbing into a Whiteout............ 89

May 27-A Very Windy Corner.................. 98

May 28-Alone in a Tent.........................105

May 29-The Basin Camp........................107

May 30-At the Edge of the World 115

May 31-Climbing the Dreaded Wall 124

June 1-A Day of Rest 129

June 2-Boredom Sets In........................ 131

June 3-To the High Camp.......................133

June 4-The Summit!.............................. 137

June 5-Resting at High Camp................. 151

June 6-Tragedy Strikes 153

June 7-Sorrowful Day at the High Camp 162

June 8-Descending the Deadly Ridge 166

June 9-Down to the Base Camp............................... 171

June 10-Stuck on Denali..176

June 11-Flying to Talkeetna.................................... 178

June 12-Home at Last.. 183

Return to the Real World 187

Climbing Again?... 200

Denali's Lasting Impression....................................203

Bibliography 209

Acknowledgements 211

About the Author.. 212

Thank You.. 212

Foreword

By Kara Hymel

When my dad asked me to write the foreword to his book, I have to admit I was daunted, but honored. He has always been a storyteller, and his adventure on Denali was the story of his lifetime.

My father's stories have been a large part of my upbringing, and, in a way, they have shaped who I am. I have grown up on these stories, retold them for years, and even made some of them my own to entertain my high school students. I put writing this forward off for months. It wasn't because I had forgotten about it or had too much to do; it just seemed to be a difficult task. Anyone who knows me at all knows about my close connection with my dad, and sitting down and putting our relationship into words seemed tough. To illuminate the effect of my dad's stories is to describe the impact of his life on mine, and that seems nearly impossible. But here goes.

It's rare to consider your dad an actual best friend, but I can honestly say that I do. He has the ability to take any problem and find the best solution to it, and his highly logical manner always tempers my tendency to have overly emotional reactions to difficult circumstances. He has supported me through so much, and often if I had troubles, he was the only one I felt I could turn to. He was the one who helped me accept that certain things weren't my fault and that bad things are often a part of life. Whenever I'm faced with a bad situation, he teaches me to see the light through the darkness, and I think he truly learned how to do that through his experiences on Denali.

To help you understand the kind of person my dad is, you have to understand his humor. Humor is at the center of my relationship with my dad. He makes me laugh on a daily basis, and his stories are funny to me every time I hear them no matter how many times I have heard them. I distinctly remember eating in the K-Mart Eatery when I was in high school. My dad was telling a bunch of his classic stories, and we were both laughing the entire time, oblivious to the others around us. As we paid for our meal, an elderly woman who was sitting across the restaurant approached us. She said, "I've never seen two people enjoy each other so much. It was wonderful seeing how much fun you have together." That was the moment I knew my relationship with my dad was special, that not everyone had a dad that they truly enjoyed being with. Simply watching my dad watch his favorite TV shows brings other people around him joy; he has been known to break into knee-slapping, uncontrollable guffaws at an episode of "Seinfeld" he has seen 20 times. Watching him laugh makes me laugh. It's so easy to be cynical today, but my cynicism is defenseless against my dad's laugh. It shows me that pure joy is alive and well, and life is enjoyable if you make it enjoyable. It shows me that maybe, in fact, that glass is half-full, no matter how dreary and dull life can seem.

I've only heard my dad talk about his experience on Denali a handful of times. It seems difficult for him to talk about, as it is for me to hear about. I was somewhat blissfully unaware of the entire situation as it happened because I was in Jamaica on a mission trip. The only news I received was that someone in my dad's team died and they didn't know who, which was obviously very distressing. Upon my return, I really only knew that something bad had happened and my dad was somewhat different because of it. He wasn't depressed or distant; you could just tell he'd been through hell and was working through a range of emotions. When he was finally able to share his experience, he showed me that tragedy can and will touch our lives and that resilience and strength comes from overcoming such heartbreak.

My dad is financially stable and professionally successful, but his true success is the way he lives his life. He embodies integrity, wit, and empathy, and I am fortunate to have him as a part of my daily life. Because of him, I choose to enjoy life, to embrace the weird situations in life, and never to succumb to simply going through the motions. I hope you enjoy his story as much as I have.

Author's Introduction

Pinned by the wind to the steep icy flanks of Denali, my ice axe in a death grip and my legs shaking from the exertion of holding my body fast by the points of my crampons, I struggled to comprehend how I could have gotten into this jam. When just two days earlier I had stood jubilantly on the highest peak of North America, now I was paralyzed in fear, wondering whether I would live or die. I became aware of distant voices struggling to be heard above the din of the wind. Then I heard the scream...

We all have a story to tell, and this is mine; this is my epic adventure. I climbed Mt. McKinley, now officially known by its native name, Denali, in 1998, as a client on a guided expedition. The events that occurred on the climb dramatically affected my life, forcing me to face the full range of human emotions. The experience was both immensely rewarding and tragically heartbreaking.

It took me a long time to write this account. Soon after the trip, I was compelled to tell the story. It is one that plays over and over again in my mind, much like the tune or dream that can't be forgotten. Perhaps, I thought, it will help me to tell others. Immediately after my expedition, I began writing, but my efforts fizzled to a halt. Although I always wanted to complete writing my account of the climb, I filed my notes away where they lay dormant for many years. Coming across them when I moved, I read what I had written. Prompted by the urgings of my supportive wife, I decided to finish the project.

Now, I am glad that it took me so long to write. Initially, I thought that no one would be interested in reading an account of a climb of Denali that happened nearly twenty years ago. Although I am forgetful of many things in life, this story seems as fresh to me as if it had happened yesterday. But now, looking back, I see things in a wholly different and enlightened perspective. The passage of time has allowed me greater insight into my thoughts and feelings. As this one did, some meals take longer to cook than others, but I hope the meal is all the more tasty.

I also realized that a climb of Mt. McKinley is a timeless event. Undoubtedly, equipment has improved over time, but the paths to the top are essentially the same, and the mountain continues to exist as it has for eons.

The name of the mountain has recently changed. Much to the chagrin of Ohioans who feel that President McKinley's good character has been slighted, the name was officially changed from Mt. McKinley to its native name of Denali. When I wrote this, I referred to the mountain by both names, and have left it that way. Also, the mountain has shrunk by ten feet; recent more accurate summit measurements have shown that Denali's height is ten feet less than the previous calculation of 20,320 feet, which was done in the 1950's.

My adventure on Mt. McKinley had a dramatic impact on me, and, consequently, my life. In a way, I was a different person afterward. The footprints of my journey through life are stamped with the imprint of this adventure. All of my successes and failures are, in some intangible way, partly the result of the impression this expedition had on me. It is easier to describe the factual events of this expedition than it is to find the words to adequately describe the influence it had on my life. I do my best here, but worry that I fall short of the mark.

This is not an account of a climb written by a professional mountaineer, nor is it a guidebook. This is the story of a person who participated in mountaineering as a diversion, only for selfish amusement. Mountaineering is something that I enjoyed doing once or twice a year to get away from the daily grind and to find some challenge and excitement; I was a "weekend warrior," as amateur enthusiasts are often called. This is more an account of my adventure there and the impact that it had on my life.

Why climb mountains? It is a question that has been asked for as long as people have engaged in such activities. Mountaineering literature contains some of the best writing that you will ever encounter. It is replete with reflections on this subject. George Leigh Mallory, a member of an early British team attempting a climb of Mt. Everest, when asked why he endeavored to do so, uttered the now famous response, "Because it is there." I, too, attempted to find the answer to that question. Perhaps in doing so I might better understand my own needs, or, more accurately, my compulsion to participate in an activity that more practical people might label as nonsensical.

A climb of Denali, particularly one such as mine, places everything into perspective. The motivation for climbing is better understood. But such understanding raises other questions: Is it worth the risk? Is it worth the sacrifice?

The extraordinary author Jon Krakauer, in the book "Into Thin Air," a personal account of the 1996 tragedy on Mt. Everest, wrote "There were many, many fine reasons not to go, but attempting to climb Everest is an intrinsically irrational act--a triumph of desire over sensibility." Search as we may, however, there might be no rational explanation for the yearning to climb mountains.

Thus, these are my reflections on a mountaineering adventure that had a profound impact on my life. In a bigger sense, this is the story of my extraordinary life.

A journey of a thousand miles must begin with a single step.

Lao Tzu

The Seeds are Planted

Most people would have considered me to be a practical person. I was a small town attorney in Central Florida, one member of a two-lawyer firm, where I had practiced law for many years. Having a wife and three wonderful children, as well as parents and siblings in the area, my life was centered on family and work. I was a member of a church and an active participant in several civic organizations. For all intents and purposes, I was a regular guy who lived a normal, quiet, perhaps sedentary life.

I have been interested in mountaineering ever since I was a youngster. I treasured books and stories on mountaineering and delightfully poured over photographs of mountains. Sir Edmund Hillary has always been one of my idols. Hillary, a beekeeper and mountaineer from New Zealand, and Tenzing Norgay, a Nepalese Sherpa, became the first to reach the summit of Mt. Everest in 1953. I still have vivid memories of a photograph of the ruggedly handsome Hillary, after having summited Everest, sipping a cup of hot tea, a broad smile on his bearded face, with eyes hidden behind dark goggles, very delighted and obviously exhausted.

To me, there was no greater adventure. I particularly enjoyed stories of the conquests of the world's greatest mountains--Everest, K-2, Mt. McKinley and the like. As much as I enjoyed the subject, I never really saw myself as a participant in these adventures.

I grew up in the beautiful countryside of northeastern New Jersey. Although it was a rural area, it was only a 45 minute drive to New York City. I am the oldest of seven children. My father was a Captain on the police department, and he was well-known and respected in the area. My mother kept busy raising us while working clerical and waitress jobs to help make ends meet. She cooked and cared for us and made sure that we always had a happy home. Although we were not well-off financially, we never suffered from a lack of love and affection. We were, and are to this day, a close and loving family.

I did well in school, enjoyed reading, and studied hard. But I also loved the outdoors. We lived in a neighborhood surrounded by woods, and together with my siblings and friends, I spent a great deal of time hiking and playing there. There are hills in the area, which we youngsters called mountains, and I particularly relished clambering up and down them. Even as a child, I had a vivid imagination, and when I walked through the woods and trudged to the peak of one of our "mountains," I imagined myself, in the style of Walter Mitty, standing atop Mt. Everest.

Although I liked the outdoors, I was never very athletic. All of my brothers were better in sports than I, and it always gave them a good laugh when I played baseball or football with them. But we all loved hiking in the woods together.

Before we had licenses and were spoiled lazy by driving, I walked almost everywhere I went, usually accompanied by my best friend. We walked from home to the ice cream store, the convenience store, or to visit friends. It was not unusual for others to see us walking along the side of the highway, no matter whether it was in the heat of summer or the frigid cold of winter. I think that had a lasting impact on me, and I still enjoy the simple pleasures of the sights, sounds and smells encountered on leisurely strolls in the wilderness.

Although not mountaineering by any stretch of the imagination, I relished spending time in the mountains of the southeast. My family had moved to Florida, and while on a summer break from law school there, I went on a hiking trip to North Carolina with my brother, Don, who had just completed his duty with the Air Force and had enrolled in college. On a whim, we threw a small tent and some clothing into my car, jumped in, and took off to escape the oppressive heat and humidity of Florida. We arrived in North Carolina, and set up camp in the Great Smokey Mountains National Park. One morning, we loaded our backpacks with food and set off for the trail. At the trailhead, we were looking at the trail map when a park ranger approached.

"Hey guys," he said, "are you planning to hike?"

"Yes sir," we excitedly replied. "We are going to hike up this trail," we said, indicating on the map, "then over to this trail, up this mountain, eat lunch here, then hike over these mountains and be back here before dark."

He chuckled loudly and responded, "Boys, if you make it to the top of that first mountain by dark, you'll be lucky!"

Undeterred by his skepticism, we marched on. After a couple of hours of strenuous uphill stomping, including getting lost after taking the wrong trail, we hung our heads in shame and returned to the tent. I learned then that trekking in those mountains is much more arduous than I had imagined.

After I was married, my wife and I took our children, Todd, Nicole, and Kara, to the mountains of North Carolina and north Georgia for summer vacations. We loved hiking up and down the trails, then cooling off by tubing in the brisk mountain streams. I cherished our family vacations to the mountains.

In later years, my son was in the Boy Scouts, and I was able to go with him on a scout trip to the North Carolina mountains. Todd has always loved the wilderness, and that trip gave us a wonderful opportunity to bond and to share in the joy of outdoor activities.

From those times, I was captivated by the gentle beauty of the highlands of North Carolina and Georgia. I think my love for those mountains began then, and they continue to inspire me to this day.

My fascination with the world's great mountains continued from my childhood into adulthood. I voraciously read mountaineering books, and watched movies on the topic whenever I could find them. Once, when I went to court in Orlando, I walked over to the library afterwards and spent an hour or so browsing through the mountain adventure section, getting fully engrossed in the photographs of the world's great mountains and mountaineers. (No, I didn't bill my client for the "research" time.)

While I maintained a keen interest into my adult life, I never considered partaking in mountaineering. All of that changed in 1994. It was then that I learned about Mt. Rainier.

*Once you have traveled, the voyage
never ends, but is played out over and
over again in the quietest chambers. The
mind can never break off from the
journey.*

Pat Conroy

Climbing Fever

Mt. Rainier is a 14,411 foot peak located near
Seattle, Washington. I read an article in a
local newspaper about someone I knew who
had climbed Mt. Rainier. I learned that a physically fit
individual with the proper equipment and interest
could sign on with a guide service and undertake an
ascent of Mt. Rainier in true mountaineering style. I
contacted Frank, the subject of the newspaper article,
and we met for lunch. Frank's excitement was
infectious and before I knew it, I agreed to go to Mt.
Rainier with his wife, Maggie, and Jeff, another person
from town. In July 1994, the three of us signed on for a
five-day expedition with Rainier Mountaineering, Inc.,
a distinguished guiding service located near Seattle.

Rainier Mountaineering, Inc., or "RMI," was
founded by Jerry Lynch and the renowned
mountaineer Lou Whittaker. Lou and his twin brother,
Jim, began their climbing careers in the Cascade
Mountains near their home in Seattle, Washington.
They gained reputations as strong, outstanding

climbers, often guiding climbs on Mt. Rainier. The Whittakers became climbing legends. In 1963 they were invited on an expedition to Mt. Everest; Lou declined to go, but Jim went and became the first American to reach the summit of the world's highest peak. Lou Whittaker led the first successful American expedition on the north face of Mt. Everest in 1984.

I had a chance to meet Lou Whittaker once when I was at Mt. Rainier, where he was guiding a private group. I was awestruck to meet such a mountaineering icon. Tall, handsome and, despite being in his mid-sixties, extremely fit, Lou was an imposing figure, but was also outgoing and friendly. Under his tutelage, RMI developed into one of the most distinguished, dependable and recognized mountain guiding services in the world.

I obtained the necessary equipment for my Rainier trip and, considering my financial investment in the gear, realized that I would certainly have to use it more than once. I also began a training program, which was a particular challenge since I was not in good physical condition. Before that, I did not maintain any regular exercise program. I was a 42 year old guy, and, other than yard work, about the only exercise I got was moving my fork between my plate and my mouth, as evidenced by my ever expanding pot-belly.

However, to prepare for my trip to Mt. Rainier, I gradually whipped myself into better shape. After several months of jogging, training on the stair master and hiking up and down hills with a heavy pack, I felt that I was ready for the task.

Arriving at Mt. Rainier, we met our guide from RMI, Phil Ershler. Phil is one of the leading mountain guides in the world, and it was an honor for me to be a part of his group. We spent the night in the beautiful and rustic Paradise Inn located at the base of the peak. That night, as I nervously attempted to sleep, I was haunted by the sound of the wind howling across the building. I imagined being on Rainier the next day, struggling to stay upright against hurricane-force winds, only to be blown off the mountain. I got little rest that evening.

Paradise Inn is located at an altitude of 5,400 feet. The climbing route from there goes up the south side of the mountain to the summit. We participated in the five-day program, which included significant training on rope and climbing techniques, rappelling, the use of crampons, ice axes, carabiners, and other mountaineering equipment, mountain safety training, and the proper methods to pack backpacks, set up tents, cook and eat. The trip concluded with an ascent of the summit. I was thrilled when we made it to the top.

At that time, it was the most physically demanding endeavor I ever engaged in. On the other hand, it was also one of the most rewarding. I enjoyed the experience so much I couldn't wait to go again. While I was there, I learned that there are guide services like R.M.I. available to lead trips on mountains around the world, and that there are many expeditions available even for novices like myself.

Commercial guides revolutionized the mountain climbing industry. Using guides, we "weekend warriors" have access to climbing mountains all over the globe. Guides are unique individuals; they are extremely physically fit and are skillful climbers, and possess great people skills. During expeditions, they wear many hats: cook, counselor, teacher, doctor, and navigator, to name a few. Often their skills are put to the test as they must put up with people who have no business being on a mountain. They all seem to have the patience of Job.

Phil Ershler began guiding on Mt. Rainier in 1971, and, since 1974, he has been a full-time guide. He leads mountaineering expeditions all over the world. Phil has made hundreds of successful climbs of Mt. Rainier, and over 25 successful ascents of Mt. McKinley. In 1984, Phil became the first American to summit Mt. Everest's north face. In 1989, he became one of the few individuals to have climbed the seven summits--the highest peak on each of the seven continents. In addition to being a superb climber, Phil is personable and an overall good guy.

As is so often the case in life, my dream to climb again fell into limbo and I did not do any further mountaineering for a couple of years. However, I returned to Mt. Rainier with another local friend, John, who had extensive mountaineering experience. During a particularly hot Florida summer day, John called and suggested that we get away from the heat. On a spur of the moment, we were able to connect with an R.M.I. group and completed a two-day guided ascent to the summit. This short but demanding trip is affectionately known as "the death march." The weather was beautiful, clear and so warm that we began the climb in shorts. Again, the experience was physically demanding, but standing on the summit was exhilarating, and I wanted more.

John and I returned to Mt. Rainier. We signed on with a small group of climbers John knew, to attempt an ascent on a more difficult route. Again, Phil Ershler was our guide. After a day of hard climbing, we ran into a light drizzle of rain. When we arose early the next morning, it was raining steadily. Phil studied the situation, and told us the route above was difficult and steep, and was likely frozen over. We waited awhile for the weather to improve and when it didn't, we descended. The march back down the mountain was a wet slog through a continual downpour, so we were completely soaked. We had to stop at a laundromat on the drive back to the hotel, where all of us washed our filthy wet climbing clothes. Although we did not make it to the summit, the experience was fun and I enjoyed the companionship of some wonderful fellow climbers.

In the fall of 1996, John and I went on a trip to climb two Mexican volcanos, Ixtaccihuatl and Orizaba. Once again, Phil Ershler was our guide.

In Mexico, John and I joined a group of about nine other climbers. Most of them had climbed Mt. Rainier and had a fair amount of climbing experience, and they also knew Phil from previous ventures. This was my first climbing trip outside of the United States, and the cultural experience of visiting Mexico was fantastic. We spent about three days on Ixta, and two on Orizaba. The climbing was somewhat more vigorous than Rainier, and the additional altitude, with Ixta at 17,700 feet and Orizaba at 18,800 feet, was a challenge. It was enjoyable climbing in this environment with these more experienced and spirited climbers. The trip to Mexico was very gratifying, and it fueled my desire to continue climbing. Honestly, I was hooked. All I could think about was my next climb. Where would I go?

Does the road wind up-hill all the way?
Yes, to the very end.
Will the journey take the whole long day?
From morn to night, my friend.

Christina G. Rossetti - *Up-Hill*

Denali Dreaming

I set my sights on Denali. I talked with John and Frank about my idea for an expedition to Mt. McKinley. Frank had been there a couple of years earlier and was brokenhearted to have failed to reach the summit. He was in excellent physical condition and, although he was strong enough to complete the summit attempt, the expedition was beset with bad weather. His team spent many days confined to tents, and they were ultimately forced down without a summit bid.

John had better luck. His group spent a longer time on the mountain with good weather conditions for the summit attempt. They reached the top. John said it was one of the most gratifying experiences of his life.

Mt. McKinley is located in Alaska approximately 200 miles north of Anchorage. Now officially known by its native name of "Denali," it is a massive granite dome lying beneath huge glaciers. Mt. McKinley is part of the immense Denali National Park.

Both John and Frank related exciting tales of their Denali expeditions. My imagination was fired, and I wondered whether I was capable of such a venture. McKinley would be a substantial step up from my previous climbs. I spent a long time dwelling on it, and then broached the subject with my family. This, as you might imagine, was not easy.

My wife and children were aware that mountaineering was dangerous. It was hard to keep that a secret, particularly in light of the well-publicized disaster on Mt. Everest that happened a couple of years earlier. During two days in May, 1996, eight climbers lost their lives making summit attempts when a vicious blizzard battered Mt. Everest. The dead and injured included well-known mountaineers, guided clients and celebrities, and the press coverage was pervasive. My family had heard all about it, and voiced their concerns. However, I promised them that I would be cautious and safe. Seeing how excited I was about the project, they couldn't object too vociferously. Ultimately, I decided to go.

First, I had to consider which guide service to sign on with. Anyone without substantial mountaineering experience would be foolhardy to attempt such a trip without a reputable guide. I considered either Phil Ershler or one of the guides with Rainier Mountaineering. Actually, Phil also worked with RMI, so they were connected. Phil made one trip to Denali, near the end of May, and RMI had several trips scheduled throughout the summer. The cost of Phil's trip was somewhat higher, but he took a smaller group and he had an outstanding record of success on Denali, having reached the summit more than twenty times. I liked him and knew how he led his expeditions, so I decided to try to go with Phil.

I contacted him and was disappointed to learn that he limited his groups to four climbers and had no openings on his McKinley trip. I considered contacting RMI, but before I did Phil called and told me that it turned out that he did have an opening with his group. I quickly agreed to sign on with Phil.

Actually, I felt quite privileged to have been invited to join Phil's contingent. I knew that he would consider each member's climbing ability and personality. Phil would expect each participant in his group to be strong enough for the expedition and to have the temperament to get along with others in difficult circumstances. I was honored that Phil believed that I was compatible.

From the time that I had made my commitment to join Phil's expedition, there were approximately nine months until the departure date. I had a lot of work to do.

In preparation for the expedition, there were several areas that I had to concentrate on: developing a physical conditioning program so that I would be fit for the climb; obtaining all of the necessary equipment and gear; arranging my work schedule to take time off for the trip; and acquiring the funds to pay for the expedition. Although I paid careful attention to all of those details, I was still not prepared for what was to come.

This expedition would be a real challenge. To describe Denali as an impressive mountain is an understatement. Standing almost four miles (20,310 feet) above sea level, it is the tallest mountain in North America. It is understandable why the natives of central Alaska named it Denali, meaning "the Great One." It rises almost 18,000 feet from its tundra base, giving it the greatest vertical relief of any mountain in the world. It is located at 63 degrees latitude, and of all the mountains on earth higher than 20,000 feet, it is the northernmost one. All of this, together with its closeness to the Gulf of Alaska, gives Denali one of the most punishing climates on earth.

The weather on Mt. McKinley is severe and unpredictable. The sun can reflect brightly from the snow and ice, making a climber uncomfortably hot. More often, though, the problem is the cold and wind. Temperatures well below zero are the norm, and the peak is often buffeted by hurricane force winds. There are stories of winds so strong that they have shredded climbers' tents. Denali has the reputation of being the coldest mountain on earth. The climbing season on McKinley runs from May through July. Earlier than that the weather is too cold, although several extremely hardy individuals have done winter ascents.

The first successful winter ascent of Denali was accomplished in 1967 by Art Davidson, Dave Johnston and Ray Genet. They were part of a larger group, one of whom fell into a crevasse and was killed early in the expedition. After reaching the summit, they encountered a storm on the descent. At about 18,000 feet, the climbers built a small snow cave and hunkered down to ride out the blizzard. As temperatures dropped and the days passed, with very little food and water, the three thought that they would perish in an icy grave. The wind chill dropped temperatures to as low as minus 148 degrees, while inside their snow cave it was as cold as 35 below zero. After six days, the frostbitten climbers were able to clamber out and descend, barely surviving before reaching their teammates below. It was a miracle that they lived. Obviously, a winter expedition is not in the cards for me.

Climbing later in the summer is also problematic. After mid-July, the melting of the snow on the lower part of the mountain creates additional and more deadly crevasses, which are open gaps in the glacier, making it very difficult and sometimes impossible for climbers to circumnavigate them and for the transport planes to land on the glacier. Thus, the optimum climbing season is a window of only two and a half months from May to July. Considering the great number of climbers from around the world attempting the ascent, it means that there are many people on the mountain in this short period of time.

A climber on Denali faces not only extreme weather conditions, but other obstacles such as crevasses and avalanches. Adding to the difficulty is the massive size of the mountain. Distances are deceptive, and climbing parties must carry large amounts of gear and food to survive the length of time that an expedition takes. The distance from Base Camp to the summit is about seventeen miles, but the trip is actually much longer. Climbing parties must ferry food and supplies up the mountain and place them in caches, or snow pits. By digging a hole into the snow, placing food and equipment into it, and then covering the items with snow, climbers create these "caches." The caches are marked with tall bamboo wands so that they can be located after heavy snowfalls. After caching supplies, the climbers then return to stay the night at the lower altitude camp, later returning to pick up some of the cached items and then moving them up to a higher campsite, while leaving some behind for the descent. Thus, in going up and down the mountain in this fashion, an expedition will cover a substantial amount of distance in making a summit attempt.

Although the standard route up the mountain, known as the West Buttress, is not considered by climbers to be technically difficult, the lower part of the route is strewn with crevasses, often hidden, while the upper part is steep and very exposed. Even though we were taking the standard route, I knew that it would be an incredible challenge. The success rate for reaching Denali's summit via the West Buttress route is about 50%.

It was with this background that I embarked upon my mission. I faced the upcoming challenge with excitement and trepidation, both of which grew as the expedition drew nearer.

Training for a climb is always difficult. It is a problem finding time for workouts. I stayed busy with my law practice, and often worked sixty hour weeks. Also, family commitments demanded time. I particularly enjoyed activities with my wife and youngest daughter, our last child residing at home, and always felt guilty working when I should have been at home. Yet I knew that undertaking an expedition like McKinley without being in top physical condition would be a serious mistake.

I began training in earnest about eight months ahead of our scheduled expedition. As I knew from previous trips, the closer the departure date, the more anxious I became about physical conditioning, but it is difficult to stay focused on a goal so many months away. I had been keeping up with a running program with varying degrees of seriousness; I had entertained thoughts of entering a marathon well before I decided on the Denali expedition, and had worked on gradually increasing my running distance for that, but I had never gotten comfortable with a marathon-like distance. I established a fairly regular schedule of running three miles every other day, and then a longer distance, such as five to ten miles, on Sundays. Since it gets incredibly hot in the afternoons in Florida, I did my running in the early morning hours.

Weight lifting had never been my forte, but I decided to go out in the garage and dig out the set of weights that were buried there in an attempt to increase my muscle mass. I dusted off my old set of barbells and worked out on the weights every other day. My goal was to gradually increase the weight that I was lifting so that I would build up the muscles in my legs and upper body.

Exercising with a backpack on is an important part of a mountaineering training program. Most of the time climbing is spent saddled with packs containing various amounts of weight. On previous climbs of Mt. Rainier, we carried about 35-40 pounds of gear in our packs, and sometimes less. It would be different on Denali, where we would each be responsible for carrying over 100 pounds of gear, which we could split between a backpack and a plastic sled which is dragged behind the climber.

It is difficult to properly train for a climb without hiking up and down steep terrain, which is hard to find in Florida. Most of the state is at sea level and very flat, making it a challenge to find an appropriate area to practice mountain climbing. We do have several hills in our area. Although not mountains by any stretch of the imagination, they provide some areas of drops and rises in altitude sufficient to allow a good workout. One of these, a road aptly named Thrill Hill, is actually a large sink hole that drops steeply down and rises abruptly back up. You can feel your stomach drop, and create quite a scare for your passengers, if you drive quickly down the hill. Another area, that surrounding Sugar Loaf Mountain, has roads that rise and fall in varying degrees of steepness. Bicycle riders often take on the challenge of peddling up Sugar Loaf Mountain. Although I have never tried that, it looks daunting. I headed out early each Saturday or Sunday morning and hiked up and down along one of these roads with my backpack on. Over the weeks, I gradually increased the amount of weight in my pack until I was able to comfortably carry 90 pounds. I also increased the amount of time that I hiked, from about one hour until I could go for four or five. One Sunday morning while hiking up and down along these hills, my brother, Don drove past me as he was returning from an overnight campout with his daughters. He slammed on his brakes and backed up his truck. "Larry," he yelled, "is that you?" "We thought it was a homeless guy!" Although this type of training was true drudgery, and often embarrassing, it is much like actual climbing. I believe it is the best training for an expedition-style climb.

Over the months leading up to the trip, I continued my physical training program with growing sincerity as the departure date drew nearer. I also grew more concerned as that time approached; when training for these trips, I am always afraid that I will lack the physical stamina to keep up with the group. I was particularly worried about this for the upcoming Denali expedition because it was a small group and a physically demanding climb. We would be very dependent upon each other; one person's failure to perform could cause problems for the entire group. I did not want my lack of physical conditioning to cause difficulties during the climb, for me or any of the other climbers. Since there is no objective standard to determine whether or not one's physical condition is appropriate for a McKinley expedition, I was constantly anxious about this.

It seems logical that those of us living at sea level are at a distinct disadvantage for climbing at higher altitudes, and that climbers who live and train at higher places, such as in Colorado, are more fit for climbing high mountains. However, from previous experience, I found that is not necessarily the case. High altitudes affect climbers differently; some have difficulty with altitude all the time, and others handle it extremely well, but have occasional bouts of altitude illness. So even though training at higher altitudes may be beneficial in other respects, such as with acclimatizing, climbers from the lowlands do not react to higher altitudes much differently than others.

However, there is one distinct advantage of training at higher altitudes: the cold. No matter how many hills I could find, cold weather is rare in Florida. Many climbers, in preparing for cold mountain expeditions (Denali being one of the coldest), will go to extremes to prepare. They will take cold showers, sit in baths of ice, or hike nearly naked in cold, snowy weather. Although I would be at a disadvantage when it came to the cold, I did not consider doing any of those things, and hoped that I would be able to adjust to the frigid weather when I needed to.

In addition to my physical training, I continued making the other necessary preparations for the expedition. I reviewed the list of equipment that Phil Ershler sent to make sure that I had everything required. The list was quite impressive. It included: expedition boots (double plastic outer boots with soft inner boot liners), several pairs of wool socks, long-johns, pile pants, a Gore-Tex jacket and pants, a down jacket and hood, wool hat, baseball cap, polypro liner gloves, wool gloves, heavy synthetic mitts, ski goggles, sunglasses, Thermarest pad, ensolite pad, a sleeping bag rated to 20 degrees below zero, large backpack, several nylon stuff sacks, ice axe (a pointed pick used to stop falls or slides), crampons (sharply pointed metal devices to slip on the bottom of the boots to secure footing on ice and snow), snowshoes, ski poles, carabineers (oblong metal devices that snap open and closed, used to hook items to or to pass ropes through), mechanical ascenders(devices attached to ropes to help climb out of crevasses or up steep walls of ice or snow), seat harness (a belt worn around the waist and crotch to attach climbing ropes), water bottles, eating utensils, Swiss army knife, Bic lighter, nylon cord and webbing, and large trash bags. In addition, we were told to bring snack items such as GORP (a mixture of nuts and candies, like M&Ms), candy bars, crackers, and beef jerky, and items such as sun screen, lip balm, toilet tissue, personal medications, first aid items, books and a radio.

I had already acquired most of the equipment for previous expeditions, but because the weather on Denali is so cold and harsh, there were other items that would only be used on mountains like McKinley or those in the Himalayas, and I needed to get that equipment. Luckily, I had John and Frank to help. In addition to their valuable advice about the type of gear needed for Denali, Frank loaned me some of his equipment, the most important of which was his heavy down jacket.

Aside from the equipment that we had to bring, Phil provided the group gear, which included nylon expedition tents, stoves, fuel, ropes, sleds and all food other than our personal snacks. It didn't take me long to realize that we would each be carrying a heavy load of personal and group gear. It would be a challenge to minimize the weight yet assure that I did not leave anything essential behind. Over the course of the months leading up to the trip, I had many conversations with Frank and John to address this challenge, and their assistance was instrumental.

Phil provided us a list of the people in our climbing group, with their names, addresses and telephone numbers. Including me, there were a total of four climbers. One of them, Dennis, lived in Georgia, and I contacted him by phone. I learned that he had been to Denali before, but had not made it to the summit because of bad weather. He suggested that I visit him so that he could tell me about the expedition and share his insight. I did so, and Dennis was particularly helpful in advising me about equipment. He looked over my gear and showed me what he was bringing, which assisted me greatly. Thus, I felt that I was well prepared concerning my equipment needs for the trip.

One of the more difficult aspects of planning for this venture was arranging my affairs at work. This was the longest period of time that I would be absent from my office. Since the expedition was scheduled to take between two and three weeks, I wanted to assure that ample time had been blocked out on my office calendar for time on the mountain and travel to and from Alaska, so I set aside one month. In the past, I had not taken more than two continuous weeks away from my office, and in those rare instances, I was usually available by phone.

This facet of my planning caused me as much apprehension as anything else. On this trip, there would be very little opportunity for me to call my office or for my staff to contact me in the event of an emergency, especially while we were on the mountain. My law partner was available to cover any emergencies that came up, which made me feel more comfortable. Also, my office staff was competent and well prepared for my absence. It was difficult to ensure that my calendar was kept open for that length of time, particularly for litigation matters that had to be scheduled, such as court hearings, depositions or mediations. My assistants and I constantly juggled the schedule to keep this time open, and it was an ongoing problem up until the day that I left. Finally, just before my departure, I reviewed each of my pending files and place notes in them as to what should be done if matters arose during my absence, and this proved to be an onerous and time-consuming task.

Another part of my expedition planning process involved gathering the funds necessary to pay for the trip, which was no small expense. First, there was the cost of the guide service. Phil provided our guides, the food and group gear during the trip, one night of hotel lodging before and after our time on the mountain, transportation between Anchorage and Talkeetna, Alaska, and the flight from Talkeetna to the Base Camp on Mt. McKinley. Of course, this was the most expensive item associated with the trip. I also had to pay the cost of airline tickets for travel from Orlando, Florida to Anchorage, Alaska and back, and for the hotel in Anchorage. There was the additional equipment that I had to purchase, the most costly of which was a new heavy-duty down sleeping bag, since the bag that I had was insufficient. Of course, there are other travel expenses, such as meals and gift purchases.

I paid the guide service fees in a couple of installments, as Phil required, and obtained my airline tickets as far in advance of the departure date as I could. I acquired the remaining items of equipment over a period of several months as funds permitted. As the expedition approached, I grew increasingly nervous about finances; although I anticipated being gone from home for no more than three weeks, I wanted to make certain that all of my household bills were paid for one month in case I was gone that long, and to assure that my wife had monies available for her and my daughter in my absence. I became frantic two weeks before my departure, fearing that a financial disaster would happen while I was gone. More than once I considered canceling the trip, then convinced myself that it was a "once in a lifetime experience" and that I should forge on. On one of those occasions, feeling extremely guilty about leaving my family for my own enjoyment while they sat home and suffered, I told my wife that I was not going. She told me "You're going! Somehow we will find a way to get through whatever happens, and you are not going to give up on this opportunity." Her wisdom prevailed.

As the months preceding the expedition rolled by, my level of excitement grew, notwithstanding my continued concern for my family and law practice. I received information periodically from Phil, each time reading and re-reading his communications with curiosity and anticipation.

When I first signed on, Phil told me about the other climbers in our party. Mike and Meegan, a couple in their mid-twenties, lived in Denver, Colorado. Dennis, who lived in Fitzgerald, Georgia, was in his early fifties. Phil described each of them as a strong climber with a good personality. Given the length and severity of this expedition, and the fact that we would be more or less dependent upon each other throughout, I knew that Phil would be certain to put together a group of climbers who were compatible both in personality and ability.

Dennis, who was to be my tent mate, had climbed several times with Phil in the past, and had attempted Denali with Phil's group a few years earlier. Unfortunately, bad weather set in and stranded them at the High Camp and they did not reach the summit, so Dennis wanted another chance. I would come to know Dennis much better in the time prior to departing for Alaska.

I knew little about Mike and Meegan. They lived in Colorado and were engaged to be married. Mike had climbed with Phil on Mt. Rainier, and Phil described Mike as a big, strong climber. Phil had not climbed with Meegan before, but from what he knew about her, he felt that she was as tough a climber as Mike.

There is always some apprehension on these trips about others in the party. On most expeditions, the group is large enough that one or two jerks won't make much difference. On the Denali expedition, we were a small team, and that could pose a problem. Of concern to me as much as personality types were the relative strengths and abilities of the climbers. Further, and equally important, is team morale. We would have to cooperate and work together as a team under difficult and stressful circumstances. The success of our expedition, and more significantly, our lives and well-being, depended upon it. I knew, however, that Phil had taken that into account in assembling our group.

As I said, my physical preparedness for these expeditions always caused me trepidation, and I found that to be particularly true for this one. I worried constantly about faltering or not being able to keep up with the group. I knew that once the climbing started, it would be too late to do anything about those fears. However, I knew that Phil must have believed that I had sufficient mountaineering skills and aptitude to fit in with the other climbers.

After having several telephone conversations with Dennis, we received an invitation to visit him and his wife in Georgia. My wife, youngest daughter, and I drove up to his home for a weekend. Aside from his advice about my climbing gear, Dennis provided valuable insight on the mountain and the expedition.

Whenever climbers get together, climbing becomes the dominant topic of conversation. Often, the nonclimbing partners feel ignored and left out of the exchange. I knew that my wife had been through this several times before, and I admired her efforts to appear interested in climbing stories that she had heard many times over. I didn't know whether Dennis's wife was involved in climbing, but I worried that our wives would lose patience listening to Dennis and I talk mountaineering for two days. It was a great relief for me to learn that she was a wonderful person and had no interest in climbing herself, although she was also generally supportive of her husband's pursuits.

Nonclimbing partners are faced with a dilemma. Although they want to encourage their spouses, they worry about the dangers and sometimes face criticism from others. Often people will ask them how they can allow their spouses to climb. Although my choice of hobby posed some problems for my wife early on, I think that she came to understand my desire and need to do this. She did not encourage me to go climbing, but neither did she discourage me. To have someone say to her, "Why do you let him do that, he'll kill himself," was very disturbing both to her and me, because it is difficult enough to understand, let alone to convince someone else to comprehend a spouse's motivation for climbing. I know that she worried about the dangers, although we rarely spoke about it, other than for me to give assurances that I was climbing as safely as possible. We reached a level of quiet understanding that provided us some comfort, although it bothered me that she had to deal with other people's doubts and discouragement.

Mountaineering is truly a selfish sport. Any pleasure my family or friends derived from it was incidental to mine. I imagine it's much like someone watching me eat an entire chocolate cake; perhaps that person gets some pleasure from my happiness. Probably very little, though.

My choice of hobby also affected the other members of my family. I have always been close with my children, as well as my parents and siblings, and they often discussed their apprehensions about my climbing. My parents were frank and open about their concerns for me and my family. They had good reasons to be apprehensive about my climbing.

Years ago, when I was a new college student, my sister, Judy, tragically died in an automobile accident while I was away at school. Her vehicle skidded down an icy bridge and crashed into another car. She was a beautiful person, just a high school student at the time, and the loss of her life had a profoundly sad effect on our family. Although we have a large family, I know that my parents did not want to suffer the loss of another child.

I love my family dearly, and certainly did not want to do anything that would cause any of them grief. The best I could do was to assure them that I would be careful and take every precaution.

We thoroughly enjoyed our visit with Dennis and I found that he and I were compatible, which was important since we would be spending so much time together on Denali, much of it in our tent. Dennis had considerable climbing experience, having climbed Mt. Rainier, Mt. Elbrus in Russia, and a couple of peaks in South America, to name a few. More importantly from my perspective was the fact that Dennis had made an attempt to climb Denali several years ago with Phil. He was able to help me tremendously with his advice concerning gear, logistics, and details of the climb.

Dennis told me, "You'll never be as hot, and you will never be as cold as you will be on this trip." He warned me about countless dreary hours spent trapped in tents waiting out storms. He told me about the unsurpassed beauty of the mountain.

Before we left Dennis's home, he offered to lend me several items of essential equipment, including a pair of snowshoes and a large duffel bag, and showed me how to separate my gear into various sized nylon sacks. We made plans to meet in Anchorage and to share a hotel room there. As we returned to Florida, I reflected on our visit with Dennis, and was glad that I had gotten to meet him before our expedition began. I looked forward to the Denali expedition with renewed excitement, but also with a heightened concern for its seriousness.

I received a message from one of my other traveling companions, Mike, about an assignment that his sixth grade science class had started. A letter from his students in Colorado arrived shortly thereafter. It explained that the class was participating in a project about mountaineering during our expedition. At the time, I did not know how great an impact that this school project would come to have.

The letter explained that the students were setting up a website, that Mike would carry a satellite phone on the trip so that he could send daily reports from the mountain, and that the students could then post the information on their website. The website would include profiles about the expedition members, and information about mountaineering and Mt. McKinley.

Thus, people from around the world could learn about and follow our expedition, while the students participated in a "virtual classroom." I was somewhat dubious about this; on one hand, it would be interesting for my friends and family to follow along with us, but if there were problems, I didn't want them overly concerned by what they learned on the students' website. I filled out the resume form they sent me so that they could publish the information as part of the climbers' profiles.

Before leaving for Alaska, I had an opportunity to visit the website. I went to my father's house and he located the site on his computer. It was really a special moment that I shared with my dad. A few years before, he had serious heart problems and suffered a stroke that had partially incapacitated him. He spent more time on his computer after that, and he particularly enjoyed "surfing the net." Although he was well aware that I was embarking on the Denali expedition, he never truly understood what was involved until he visited the students' website. There, he saw the information that the students had posted: photographs of the mountain, a visual description of the route, the itinerary, the equipment list, and a history of climbing on Denali. Thus, he gained some deeper understanding of what the expedition was all about. As we looked with excitement at his computer monitor, I silently thanked Mike's young students for putting this together.

As I continued to make final preparations for the trip, I scheduled an appointment to see our family doctor for the physical that was required for all climbers. My doctor told me I was due for a complete physical anyhow, so he set me up for the whole works.

When I looked at the form "Physician's Certificate" that the doctor was required to complete, it brought home the seriousness of the climb. The form stated:

> The bearer plans to participate in expeditionary mountaineering in Mt. McKinley National Park, Alaska. In the interest of personal safety, the National Park Service wishes to be assured that he/she is in physical and mental condition to endure the extreme stresses associated with arctic mountaineering.

> The climber will be carrying heavy loads (often 60-90 lbs.) at altitudes between 10,000 and 20,000 ft. Conditions vary from intense snow glare with temperatures as high as 90 degrees F to storms with winds of over 100 mph and temperatures of 40 degrees F below zero. Expeditions usually last from 2-4 weeks. Prolonged confinement within cramped tents or snow caves due to bad weather often occurs. Rescue may be exceedingly slow and uncertain in case of serious injury or illness.

> Headache, irritability, sleeplessness, periodic breathing, anorexia, nausea, meteorism, sore muscles and intense fatigue are common during high climbs on Mt. McKinley. More serious problems

include cold injury (particularly to feet), snow blindness, retinal hemorrhage, cerebral edema causing ataxia, stupor, and coma, and high-altitude pulmonary edema. In addition, injuries due to falls, avalanches, and fires in tents may occur.

Sounds like fun. After reading that, I wondered whether I was making a huge mistake.

There is no question that Denali can be a deadly mountain. Every year, there are deaths and serious injuries. Most of the deaths on Denali are the result of un-arrested falls, followed by deaths caused by exposure, then deaths from falls into crevasses. As a matter of fact, there are over 40 dead bodies buried on the slopes of McKinley, unrecoverable even by the diligent efforts of the Park rangers.

The deadliest year in Denali's history occurred several years before my expedition. As a result of a lethal storm, eleven people perished on Mt. McKinley in 1992. Ten percent of those who attempted to reach the summit died on the mountain that year.

One of those was the famous American mountaineer Terrance "Mugs" Stump. A renowned guide on Denali, Mugs was following two clients down the South Buttress when he fell into a crevasse that collapsed on top of him. Despite the valiant effort of the climbers to rescue him, Stump was never found.

A Swiss climber died that year after suffering respiratory problems while at 14,000 feet. Two Italian climbers also perished while climbing the Cassin Ridge, one while at the 15,000 foot mark, and another at the 11,800 foot level where he had fallen. One of them dangled on a rope a thousand feet above the camp at 14,000 feet, visible to the climbers there. Three Korean climbers were also killed when they fell on the little used Orient Express route, and their bodies were discovered at 15,000 feet. They were descending from 18,000 feet, where they had been trapped by bad weather for about a week. Finally, four Canadian climbers were killed when they fell nearly 3,000 feet while attempting to traverse the Messner Couloir, while the climbers and a ranger at the 14,000 foot camp helplessly watched far below. Aside from those deaths, there were many other climbers who were injured and rescued that year. The most bizarre incident involved a Korean climber who had fallen and was trapped in a crevasse. Apparently believing that a slow death was imminent, he had repeatedly bitten his tongue to hasten the process. That didn't work, and when he was excavated from the hole by rescuers, he was covered in blood.

In a general sense, I was aware that climbing Denali was a serious venture, but it hit home to read all of the potential dangers listed in the Physician's Certificate, and to know that I was willingly subjecting myself to them. On the other hand, I thought of spending time on this majestic mountain in the company of like-minded individuals and, God willing, the chance to stand atop North America.

Luckily, everything went well with the physical and the doctor gave me a clean bill of health, with one exception. The doctor said, "Do you know you have flat feet?" "No," I responded, "I have never heard that before. Is that a problem?" The doctor told me that being flat-footed is not necessarily a drawback, although in some cases it can preclude military service. I had never had any difficulties, but wondered how it would have affected me being drafted into the army. I was in college during the war in Vietnam, and had a college deferment during that time. However, the draft was in effect, and eligible adult males were selected for service based on a lottery system using birth dates. Unfortunately, I was not on the winning side of the lottery, and my draft number was nine, meaning I would in all likelihood be drafted. I was about to graduate from college and lose my deferment, so I knew that I was soon to be a goner. Thankfully, that year the draft ended, so I did not have to worry about being conscripted into the military. Whether or not my flat-feet marched through the jungles of Vietnam, I hoped they would hold up for the trudge up and down Denali.

As departure time neared, my preparation for the trip continued with increased earnest. I felt a growing excitement; after the many months of laborious planning and work, the time was almost here. The hours raced by so quickly that it seemed that I was caught up in some whirlwind beyond my control.

A couple of weeks before leaving, my wife threw a surprise party for me. I went to my law office after church on Sunday and when I came home that afternoon, there were a huge number of cars parked up and down the street. I was amazed when I entered the house. There were probably fifty to sixty family members and friends spread throughout the house and back yard. I was speechless. They were all there to wish me well on the expedition. I greatly appreciated everyone coming out to say farewell. On the other hand, I was a bit embarrassed by all of the attention, as I climbed for my own enjoyment, not to gain the recognition of others.

The departure date was May 19. I spent the weekend prior to that packing bags and finishing final details in my office. I had my backpack and two large duffel bags to carry all of my equipment. I must have re-packed those ten times over the weekend.

I prepared notes and cards for my family so that they could open them while I was gone. Fearful that the trash would be forgotten or that my daughter would not remember her lunch money, I left a list of household chores and reminders for them. My wife assured me, "I think we can handle this without you." I was sure that they could, but it made me feel important to believe that they couldn't function without me.

Not all those who wander are lost.

J.R.R. Tolkien – *The Fellowship of the Ring*

May 19-Welcome to Alaska

At long last, departure day arrived. I couldn't believe that it was time to go, and felt a certain sense of relief that I could do nothing else in preparation.

At the Orlando airport, I said my goodbyes, checked in for my flight and boarded the plane for Anchorage. As I flew across the country, I reflected on my readings about the history of mountaineering on Denali. Frederick Cook, the famed American explorer, claimed to have been the first person to reach the summit in 1906. Amid much controversy, his claim was later discredited. Oddly enough, in 1908 he contended that he was the first to have reached the North Pole, which was also proven false.

The first documented ascent of Denali's south summit, its highest peak at 20,310 feet, was achieved in 1913 by a party led by Hudson Stuck, an Episcopal priest serving as Archdeacon of the Yukon. His party navigated a route up the Muldrow Glacier and along the Northeast Ridge. Their expedition took about three months. Using primitive equipment, the party had to hike nearly 60 miles across the Alaskan tundra just to reach the base of the mountain. Even though it was summertime, the wind was blowing and the temperatures were very cold. On the evening prior to the summit attempt, it was minus 21 degrees. Wally Harper, a native Alaskan, was the first of the group to step onto the summit. Aside from pioneering a route to the summit, Hudson Stuck obtained valuable scientific information about the mountain.

Looking out the airplane window as we approached Anchorage, I was surprised to see snow-capped mountains, because I had assumed that the area around the city was fairly level. After landing, I caught the shuttle to the hotel where Dennis and I were staying. Since I had arrived early and Dennis was not due in until late that night, I spent some time walking in the area around the hotel. The weather was overcast and in the fifties, a change from the sunny, hot weather that I left behind in Florida.

There was a sporting goods store near the hotel, and I went inside to purchase a few additional odds and ends for the trip. I had intended to enjoy some authentic Alaskan cuisine, but opted for dinner in a Pizza Hut restaurant that I spotted; so much for the local fare. When I returned to the hotel, I had a fax "best wishes and good luck" message from home. I called to tell them that I had arrived safely, and then went off to bed. Since it was still light outside even at 11:00 p.m., I had to shut the curtains tightly to get to sleep.

Dennis arrived around midnight, and even though it was late, I welcomed his arrival and was glad that he had gotten to Alaska without difficulty. We passed brief greetings, then I went back to sleep, looking forward to meeting the rest of our group at the Anchorage airport in the morning.

Montani Semper Liberi

(Mountaineers are Always Free).

The motto of the State of West Virginia

May 20-On To Talkeetna

Since we had some time in the morning before meeting Phil Ershler, Dennis and I went to a nearby bookstore and spent time browsing. Dennis spotted a climbing magazine featuring an article about Mt. McKinley on the cover. We each purchased a copy, but Dennis wisely suggested that we wait until after the climb to read that article; it would have been unnerving to read a story about someone's life threatening climb of Denali at this point in our trip.

We went on to the airport and met Phil immediately upon entering the designated baggage area. With Phil was Chris Hooyman, his assistant guide, Mike and Meegan, Romulo, a climber from Ecuador, and Ellen, who was also from Colorado. Phil made hasty introductions, as he was in a hurry for us to retrieve the baggage and meet the van to transport us to the town of Talkeetna.

We met the driver of the van, a young lady from Talkeetna, and then drove a short distance to a storage facility to pick up the group gear that Phil had shipped ahead. There were many large duffel bags stuffed full of tents, food, stoves and other necessities for our trip. We loaded those on top of the van then hopped inside for the 100 mile drive from Anchorage to Talkeetna. Phil explained that the ride would take about two hours, and that we would stop at a store in a town about midway to purchase lunch and snack items for the expedition.

As we drove toward Talkeetna, we had a better opportunity to get acquainted with each other. Ellen and Romulo were Phil's friends, and although they were a separate climbing team from ours, they would be traveling on the mountain closely with our group. Romulo, I learned, was a mountain guide in Ecuador, and was somewhat of a celebrity there. He was an exceptional photographer, well-known for his mountain and outdoor photography, and he enjoyed flying Ultralight airplanes, from which he shot many of his beautiful photographs.

His English was slightly broken, but otherwise excellent. He was quick-witted and had a remarkable sense of humor. He appeared to be in his mid-thirties, thin and in excellent physical condition. Although Romulo had extensive climbing experience in the Andes, this would be his first attempt at Denali.

Ellen lived in Vail, Colorado, and worked in a health food store. She, too, appeared to be in excellent physical condition. I learned that she enjoyed mountaineering and long distance trail running, including 100 mile races. She had attempted McKinley with Phil twice before, but had awful weather conditions on both trips and failed to reach the summit.

She seemed very determined that her third attempt would have better results.

Prior to arriving in Anchorage, I had assumed that Mike and Meegan were married. However, as we traveled toward Talkeetna, I learned that they were engaged and planned to marry shortly after the expedition. Mike immediately struck me as an imposing figure; he was about 6'6" tall and very strong. Meegan, on the other hand, was tiny. I learned that she had been an extremely talented figure skater, and she certainly looked the part. Both of them were outgoing and friendly. I wondered, though, how this trip would affect their apparent close and loving relationship.

Phil's assistant guide on this trip was Chris Hooyman. His assistant guides were usually selected from those at Rainier Mountaineering, Inc., and this is where Chris worked. These personable young men and women, usually in their early twenties, are strong climbers and they work well with clients. They are sometimes college students, and often work summers as climbing guides and winters as ski instructors. Most of them have impressive climbing resumes for their relatively young ages. As assistants, they did most of the menial or grunt work and helped the lead guide care for the clients. I knew that it was an honor for a young guide to be selected as an assistant by Phil, particularly on an expedition such as this one.

Chris seemed the personification of the assistant guide. He was twenty years old, extremely fit, and very likeable. When he was nineteen, Chris became the youngest assistant guide to summit Denali. He appeared to be as excited about our expedition as we were.

As he had done on my previous trips with him, Phil responded to the many questions that were posed concerning the expedition. He spent some time describing our itinerary in closer detail. As always, I listened carefully to what Phil was saying.

As we drove toward Talkeetna, I was impressed with the evident vastness of Alaska. For mile after mile, we passed nothing but green open spaces, here and there passing a house or small town. In the distance I saw snow-capped mountains, and I kept staring out the window hoping to catch a glimpse of Denali. However, it was hidden by distant clouds and I never saw the mountain until we landed at the Base Camp.

After driving for a few hours, we arrived at Talkeetna. People I knew who had visited Talkeetna described it as a "unique" place. I had heard that this was the town that inspired the television show "Northern Exposure." The town lived up to my expectations. As we drove down the main street, we saw shops of all types, as well as fishing and guiding services, restaurants, and bars. These ran the spectrum from run-down structures that were barely standing to new, upscale buildings. People of all types were walking up and down the street. Many were middle-aged well-dressed tourists, while others were obviously mountaineers. The climbers appeared to fall into two categories: the first included those who hadn't been on the mountain yet, as evident by their smiling, happy faces and new, shiny climbing duds, while the second group consisted of those who had returned from the mountain; they looked sunburned, frail and beaten, and were clad in grungy climbing gear. The remainder of the people fit into neither group, but given their rough-hewn appearances, they were most likely locals.

We soon arrived at our hotel, a plain, one story building on the edge of Talkeetna. Phil checked in while we unloaded the gear from the van. I was amazed by the huge mountain of supplies that we had; aside from our individual backpacks and sacks were numerous large duffel bags, each heavy from the weight of the group gear packed inside. I wondered how we were going to haul all this equipment up the mountain, and whether anyone else in the group shared my concern. If others had apprehensions, they were unvoiced.

Phil led us to our rooms. Each appeared to be a similar, simply furnished unit, somehow fitting for Talkeetna. Dennis and I took our packs to our room and, following Phil's instructions, unpacked everything from them so that he and Chris Hooyman could inspect the items that we had brought along.

Chris came into our room and began working his way through the mass of equipment spread across the beds and floor, seemingly covering the entire room. He examined each item, checking through his mental list so as to assure that we had everything that we needed, and that the gear was appropriate for this expedition. The guides were well-experienced in carrying just the right type and amount of equipment. They knew that we novices always brought along too much gear, and that on a trip such as this, transporting extra weight is counterproductive. "Two pairs of long-johns will be sufficient. You won't need the third pair," he said. "Leave behind those booties; they are not warm enough. Mike may have an extra pair that you could borrow," Chris told me. He continued to inspect my gear in this manner, and I was pleased that all of my major items met with his approval.

Chris spotted a small stuffed moose that my youngest daughter had given to me to carry on this trip. She had given him to me for good luck on my first climb, and I had taken him on each expedition ever since. "Mounty," she had named him. Mounty usually wound up in the bottom of my backpack, frozen quite solid, making his way up and down the mountain with me. I was somewhat embarrassed when Chris spotted him. "Oh, that's something my daughter gave me to carry for good luck," I said, "I'll leave it behind." Chris smiled back at me. "No, you better bring that along," he said, "I know how important something like that is." I smiled back at Chris, and tossed Mounty into my backpack.

After spending some time organizing our gear, we got together to walk through Talkeetna. It is an eclectic little town. New and modern shops stood adjacent to old bars. There were guiding services for climbers and fishermen, transportation and flight services, gift shops, stores, sporting goods shops, restaurants, bars, and a couple of hotels. Many tourists walked up and down the street, mixing in with climbers and the local residents. Phil and Chris pointed out the landmarks and points of interest. We passed the National Park

Service station, a fairly new and elegant wooden structure. Phil explained that we would have to visit there to register with the Park Service before flying to Denali's Base Camp.

We ate dinner together at the restaurant at our hotel. This would be our last dinner before landing on the mountain, so everyone ate heartily. It was good to sit as a group and to get to know each other a bit better. Although we tried to hide it, I believe that we all were suffering from some pre-expedition nervousness. Phil told us that we would eat breakfast in the morning, register at the ranger station, and then go to the airport and, weather permitting, fly up to the Denali Base Camp.

Dennis and I walked behind the hotel after dinner. There was a large open area strewn with rocks. A small stream cut through the center of it. This is the Talkeetna River, and later in the summer, when the snow melts and water runs off the distant mountains and glaciers, the river will grow many times its present size, filling the now dry rock-strewn area with raging waters. I searched the horizon for a sign of Denali, but it was not to be seen. To me, it was surprising that within a forty-five minute airplane flight from this flat, sea level area, lie huge mountains, including our destination, the highest point on the continent.

My mind was full of questions. I wondered whether I was capable of the challenge, whether I was fit enough, mentally and physically, to tackle this beast. I wondered whether I was properly prepared, and whether I would make a lethal mistake even if I was able. I wondered about the things that I lacked control over, such as avalanches, crevasses, vicious storms, the deadly armaments of an angry tyrant, lying in wait for me. I wondered if maybe I was wrong, and that perhaps I imagined the mountain to be worse than it really was. Here it is, I thought, the union of the concept and the truth. I was done thinking about Denali, and soon I'd have answers to my questions.

The tops of mountains are among the unfinished parts of the globe, whither it is a slight insult to the gods to climb and pry into their secrets, and try their effect on our humanity. Only daring and insolent men, perchance, go there.

Henry David Thoreau – *The Maine Woods*

May 21-The Ascent Begins

After breakfast together, we proceeded to the National Park Service ranger station. The building was as nice on the inside as it appeared outside. There were books, postcards and photographs of Denali available for purchase. Phil registered our group with the rangers, and we each paid the required National Park Service fee. We then gathered in a small room with a couple of German climbers and a ranger. To assure that we were properly outfitted, the ranger asked each group leader questions about the equipment and supplies the group was carrying, making sure that we had essential items such as first aid kits and C.B. radios. They asked about our tents and what materials they were made from. Then the ranger proceeded to show a slide presentation on climbing Mt. McKinley, the purpose of which seemed to be to dissuade us from ascending the mountain. It focused on the substantial risks and dangers of the climb, all of which had already been drilled into my head.

We left there and went back to the hotel to pack up our gear for transport to the airport. Although the airport was on the opposite end of town from our hotel, we enjoyed the short walk while the van transported the equipment.

The Talkeetna airport consists of a small T-shaped runway, with eight or so air service offices situated along the sides. Each air service had its own building and distinctively colored planes. The planes were small four-seated Cessnas, with ski-type landing gear fitted along the wheels. As I looked around, I was overwhelmed. Here I stood among the legends of the Alaskan air, seeing the names that I had often read about--Hudson, Geeting and others. These were the rugged pilots who had come to Alaska and pioneered air travel to Denali and its vicinity, opening up the area to adventurers like me who might otherwise never come to see it. These men were known for their nerves of steel, a well-deserved reputation given the difficulty of flying in the Denali region. They were also a cast of characters who fit in well in Talkeetna.

We were flying with Geeting's air service. Phil spoke with the owner, Doug Geeting, and they concurred that the weather was fit enough for a flight to the Denali Base Camp. We went into the hanger and unloaded our equipment from the van. After that we weighed each pack and duffel bag so that the pilots would be able to load the planes appropriately. Phil explained that three of us would fly on each plane, and that we would have to load as much gear into each of them as possible. We would be cramped and it would not be a comfortable flight. As we waited for our three planes to be fueled, we went into the office, met Doug Geeting and some of his other pilots, and looked at the impressive photographs hanging on the walls. Many of those were photos of prominent climbers and other celebrities, and most of them were autographed with compliments to Doug.

In the old days prior to the use of ski planes to fly to Denali, climbers were forced to hike to the base of the mountain, a long, time consuming, and treacherous ordeal. To hike from Talkeetna to Denali's Base Camp requires one to cross at least 60 miles of mostly impenetrable, soggy muskeg and mosquito infested bogs, an unpleasant task at best. Although I have the highest admiration for those early hardy climbers who made that trip and then climbed the mountain, most of us are not up to the task and would much prefer the flight in.

Soon Doug announced that it was time to load up. Phil, Chris and Dennis hopped into the first ski-plane, and we watched as it taxied down the runway, turned, and within a few seconds it was airborne. Mike, Meegan and I jumped into the next one. Since Mike was the largest person, the pilot asked him to sit in the front seat next to him, while Meegan and I squeezed into the back. I could not believe it. Here I was, about to take off for Denali.

As the small plane struggled to gain altitude in the cloudy, gray sky above Talkeetna, I looked out of the window and saw mile after mile of green, open space. Here and there were houses hidden among the trees, but there were no towns, roads or other signs of civilization. I strained my eyes northward in the direction that we were flying, hoping to catch sight of the big mountains, but saw none. It seems as if we flew over flat, forested terrain for about fifteen minutes.

Eventually I spotted snow-covered mountains in the distance. Soon, the carpet of green forest yielded to snowy-white mountains, which gradually grew in size. Mike, Meegan and I were all amazed, each of us uttering excitedly, "Look at that!", "Wow!" or "Incredible!" as we snapped photographs from the small windows of the plane. We were surrounded by impressive steep snow-covered peaks. I felt as if our plane was an insignificant dot against this immense stone and snow background.

The sky was overcast, but visibility was fairly good. As we got into the mountains, I could tell that the wind was increasing because the plane bounced and pitched, its engine exerting itself to pull us up and forward. We were flying in between the surrounding mountains, high granite peaks on each side, appearing so close it seemed that I could reach out and touch them. We flew through "One-Shot Pass," and it didn't take too much imagination to realize where that name came from. It was the most incredible scenery that I have ever seen, and although I was nervous about the flight, the overwhelming view was awesome and captivated my attention.

Suddenly, although the engine was loudly whining and droning at a full throttle, it seemed as if we had stopped. Banking hard to the east and bouncing in the wind, we began to descend. My earlier apprehension quickly turned to fear. I focused all of my attention on the direction that we were headed. I could not see much through the front window, because the nose of the plane was turned upward. As we continued to drop, the pilot, who was earlier carrying on conversations with us, was now silent and completely focused on controlling the plane. I soon realized that we were landing, but I could not tell where. Then, off in the distance, I noted small specks of color against the white backdrop of a relatively flat, broad glacial ice pack. As we got closer, I recognized them as tents. Parallel to the tents ran a line marked with small flags--the landing strip. My heart pounded with excitement as I realized that we were about to land at the Denali Base Camp.

Our small plane bobbed along the ice and snow runway and ground to a halt. The pilot barked for us to get out, and I followed Mike and Meegan as each quickly jumped out the door. As I looked out, I was overwhelmed by the scene. There were twenty or so tents of various shapes, colors and sizes stretched out laterally along the runway. Climbers were intermingled among the tents. Some were standing and looking in our direction, apparently either watching our arrival or looking for long awaited planes for their departure. Others were busy with different chores, some fixing tents, others preparing sleds and packs for travel. My study was interrupted by a call from the pilot, who reminded us that we needed to unload our gear from the plane as quickly as possible so that he could leave. With obvious haste he threw out our packs, ice axes, crampons and other equipment. The sky was overcast and I knew that he wanted to get going to avoid being stuck here in bad weather. When our gear was unloaded in a pile clear of the plane, we assisted the pilot in turning the plane in the opposite direction for his flight out, grabbing onto the struts of the wings and pushing the plane 180 degrees. Thus situated, the pilot jumped inside, started the engine and, with a roar, he was soon bouncing along the runway in the opposite direction from our landing. I watched as the plane became airborne, groaned to gain altitude, and soon appeared as a small speck against the rock walls of the surrounding mountains.

This is the Denali Base Camp. Located on a broad, flat strip on the glacial river at 7,000 feet in altitude, it is an area free of crevasses and fairly safe from rock falls or avalanches. This is the landing strip for planes ferrying the climbers, and an area where many of them camp. During the climbing season, Base Camp was managed by Annie Duquette, affectionately known as "Base Camp Annie." For almost 10 years, living in a large permanent tent at the Base Camp, she served as ground coordinator for Talkeetna air taxis flying climbers and tourists in and out of the Base Camp. She has also functioned in many other capacities, giving advice or supplies to climbers, maintaining radio communications with climbing groups on the mountain, providing weather reports, and many other tasks. The personable Annie became an institution on Denali.

We saw Phil, Chris, and Dennis, and walked over to join them. Phil was busy arranging duffel bags onto the sleds that we would use to help transport our gear. These sleds are made of hard plastic and are designed to glide through the snow. Phil had explained to us that we would be roped together in a team, as we had been on all of my previous expeditions, and that each of us would have one of these sleds attached to the rope behind us, so that we could drag a sled loaded with equipment. We would each be responsible for carrying approximately 100 pounds of gear, which could be divided between our backpacks and sleds in whatever proportion we were comfortable with. Phil advised that it was easier for him to carry a heavier load in his pack, since the sleds have a tendency to slide from side to side and go off the hiking track, or they hit spots where they stick and require a tug to dislodge them, and they often become more of a headache than a convenience. Phil and Chris assisted us in securing the large duffel bags to the sleds as we saw Ellen and Romulo arrive. After we had secured the sleds and arranged our packs for travel, Phil laid out the climbing rope.

Some expedition teams will spend a day or two camped at the Denali Base Camp before beginning the ascent. Phil disagreed with that approach and felt that it was best to start climbing as soon as possible after hitting the mountain. Our plan was to climb 1,500 feet or so up the glacier and then set up our first camp.

Our guides checked to assure that we each were ready to start traveling, then Phil instructed us to "rope up," which meant that we secured ourselves to the climbing rope at even intervals by attaching loops on the rope to our climbing harnesses. We then put on our snowshoes. As I attempted to do so, using snowshoes I had borrowed from Dennis, I realized that I didn't know how to attach them to my climbing boots, as I had never worn snowshoes before. Phil assisted me, and eventually I was set to go. I looked around in disbelief as I realized that we were about to start climbing Denali.

Phil led our rope team. I was next, tied in about twenty feet behind Phil, with Dennis behind me. Mike, Meegan and Chris followed in that order, evenly spaced out along our rope. We are always roped up during climbs, so that if one of us has the misfortune of plummeting into a crevasse or of slipping and falling, the rest of the rope team can attempt to arrest the fall. On all of my past expeditions, we practiced self-arresting, which is a maneuver in which a climber uses an ice axe to stop himself from sliding or falling, or to hold himself firmly in place to stop a fallen climber from plunging further. Although we practiced this regularly, we hoped that we would never have to self-arrest under actual conditions; it is by no means a guarantee to avoid disaster. Practice on this trip, however, was unnecessary, as this was not a time to learn new skills.

As I said a silent prayer, I took my first step as we started our ascent of Denali. We were all wearing snowshoes, except for our guides who wore skis with skins attached to the bottoms so that they could gain traction to stride uphill in the snow. Although my first few steps were awkward, I eventually got accustomed to the snowshoes as the trip progressed. We would use them on the lower part of the mountain to help avoid sinking in the snow or falling into small crevasses. We also used ski poles to secure our balance. Up above, on the higher part of the mountain, we would abandon the snowshoes and poles and begin using crampons and ice axes.

It felt good to start moving. As we did, I thought back to all of the hard work and effort that had gone into getting this far, and I committed to put forth my best effort throughout the expedition. I warned myself to pay attention, to be careful, and to be patient and take one step at a time. I also told myself to enjoy the journey; this expedition required a great deal of sacrifice, not only by me, but by my loved ones as well, and I wanted to relish every moment.

Our path followed a straight line parallel to the Base Camp. Soon that was behind us, and the route gradually dropped and followed a downward decline. This section of the route is known as "Heartbreak Hill," so named because at the end of a long Mount McKinley expedition, climbers have to ascend this long uphill section to finish the trip. I focused on assuring that Phil's sled, which was attached to the rope in front of me, did not slide into him because of the decline. Occasionally, Phil turned to shout some instructions or to check on the team. Often, he would yell out, "You're doing great!" It really seemed as if we were. We traveled at a good, steady pace, and everyone seemed pleased that we were underway.

Based on his experience, Dennis had warned me that the first few days on this lower part of the mountain are often hot ones, caused by warmer temperatures and the white heat of the sun reflecting off the brilliant snow. As a matter of fact, he said that he had never been as hot as he had been on this part of the climb. The temperature was probably in the seventies or eighties, and I soon appreciated Dennis's wisdom. It was hot. I felt like I was in an oven. Most of us had long johns on, with Gore-Tex wind jackets and pants over them. Like me, the others were unzipping their jackets to help cool down. Because the reflection of the sun from the glacier causes serious sunburn, it was important to keep skin covered. We had maximum strength sun block on areas of exposed skin, including our faces and ears, and lip balm thickly coating our lips. We also wore hats, gloves and dark sunglasses. Even though I was hot, it was not unenjoyable and actually reminded me of training back home in the heat of Florida.

We traveled in intervals of approximately an hour to an hour and a half before stopping for rest breaks. Each rest stop was similar. We took off our backpacks and zipped up our jackets to conserve body heat, since core temperature will drop rapidly while being inactive, sat down on our packs, then drank water and ate snacks, such as candy, crackers, cheese and salami. It is important to eat and drink as much as possible on these expeditions, and particularly on Denali. Water is essential not only to replace fluids lost from strenuous activity and the low humidity, but also to assure proper functioning of the body at higher altitudes. We had to drink water copiously.

It was during these breaks that we had an opportunity to look around and appreciate the beautiful scenery that we were hiking through. Usually when we are traveling, we are focused on the path in front of us and concentrating on placing each foot in the appropriate spot, and there is little opportunity to enjoy the view. So it was during these respites that we would snap photographs, emitting exclamations such as "Amazing!" or, "That's unbelievable!" It was true: Denali was shockingly beautiful.

Striking mountain peaks surrounded us. Phil pointed out some of the named ones: Mt. Hunter, to the south, and, to the southwest, Mt. Foraker, while hidden from our view, Denali's summit rose far above to the northeast.

The path we followed is known as the West Buttress route. It is considered the standard path to the summit, easier than the other more technical and severe routes on Denali. It is the route pioneered by Dr. Bradford Washburn. A cartographer and photographer, he was one of the preeminent mountaineers in America. From the 1920s through the 1950s, he made many first ascents and established new routes in the Alaskan mountains. Dr. Washburn was often accompanied on climbs by his wife, Barbara.

Bradford Washburn devoted his life to exploring, mapping and photographing the world's highest mountains. He became the leading expert on Mt. McKinley, and during his time there, he discovered a route to the summit that traveled across the West Buttress of the mountain. I had studied his beautiful and detailed photographs of Denali in anticipation of our trip. As we proceeded up the beginning of the route, I felt a reverent respect for those early climbers like Dr. Washburn, who had walked this way, with more primitive clothing and equipment, blazing the trail that would be followed by mountaineers like me for generations thereafter.

The West Buttress route begins on the southeast fork of the Kahiltna Glacier. Running 39 miles, the Kahiltna is one of Alaska's largest glaciers. This is where the Denali Base Camp is located, at an elevation of 7,200 feet. The views of the surrounding mountain peaks along this part of the route are extraordinary. Mt. Hunter, at 14, 500 feet, dominates the view to the south. Located to the northeast of the Base Camp is Mt. Frances, topping out at 10,450 feet. Directly ahead, in a westerly direction, is Mt. Foraker at 17,400 feet. I was amazed by how near these mountains appeared; although they seemed no further from me than several hundred yards, I learned that they were miles away. In the crisp and clear Alaskan mountain air, distances are deceiving and these peaks appeared much closer than they actually were.

From Base Camp, the route descends Heartbreak Hill then curves around the base of Mt. Frances to the north. This is where the southeast fork runs into the main Kahlitna Glacier, and is an area containing numerous crevasses, so climbers must pass through it with a great deal of caution. The route gradually ascends toward Ski Hill, where it rises more sharply to an altitude of 9,700 feet. Above Ski Hill, on the upper part of the Kahlitna Glacier, one is likely to encounter more severe weather. Here the route narrows into Kahlitna Pass, a dip between the surrounding rocks and peaks through which the wind funnels. The route contours sharply to the east at this point, and rises somewhat steeply up Motorcycle Hill to an altitude of 11,000 feet. Motorcycle Hill is named for motorcycle hill climbing events that take place at altitudes such as this, but it might have been more aptly named for the noise created by the strong winds which blow through this part of the mountain.

Continuing up Motorcycle Hill, the path then turns west crossing a flat plateau to the base of the mountain's West Buttress. The point where the route curves around the southern end of the West Buttress is known as Windy Corner, which is at an altitude of about 13,500 feet. The winds through here are almost constant and can be ferocious, often reaching speeds of 100 miles per hour.

Above Windy Corner, the route passes through a broad, flatter area that contains crevasse fields, requiring climbers to exercise extreme care. At 14,200 feet, a large plateau appears. This is where the Basin Camp is located, which, after the Base Camp, is the most populated site on the mountain. The National Park Service maintains a camp here staffed with rangers during the climbing season. This is a fairly safe area as it is protected from avalanche danger and is free of major crevasses. Most climbers will spend a few days here to acclimate and to prepare for a summit bid.

From the Basin Camp, the route ascends a section of the West Buttress known as the Headwall. This is the steepest part of the climb, where the route rises 2,000 feet to an altitude of 16,200 feet. The upper 800 feet of the Headwall consists of 40-60 degree angled snow and ice, and, to secure themselves, climbers will use a rope fixed into the Headwall. The course reaches the ridge of the West Buttress at the peak of the Headwall, and then continues along this ridge line across snow, ice and rock.

The climbing along this ridge, which is technically the West Buttress for which the entire route is named, is very exposed and spectacular, with drops of several thousand feet to either side. The route winds up this ridge through sections of large boulders covered in ice and snow. Here, there is little defined path.

Near the top of the ridge line is a flat plateau, which is an area of relative safety from avalanche danger. This is the High Camp at 17,200 feet. From here, climbers will stay to stage a bid for the summit. They will try to spend as little time here as possible, waiting out the typically horrible wind and snow conditions for a break in the weather so that a summit attempt may be made. The route ascends from here up a wall to Denali Pass at 18,200 feet, where the route turns across a ridge and rises to a large, flat plateau known as the Football Field. At the end of the Football Field, the route meets the narrow summit ridge, a line that elevates steeply with great exposure on both sides, where it continues to the ultimate destination, the summit of Denali.

Bradford Washburn pioneered the West Buttress route. Prior to that, the initial climbs to the summit had all been by the same path, the one taken by Hudson Stuck on his initial summit ascent. Bradford and his wife, Barbara, had ascended to the summit by way of Stuck's route in 1947, making her the first woman to have climbed to the top of Denali. After studying photographs and participating in an extensive mapping of Mt. McKinley, Bradford Washburn noticed a safer, more direct route to the top from the west side of the mountain. The only problem was that the route required an extremely long trek in to the base of the mountain. Washburn realized that could be avoided by landing a plane on the relatively safe Kahiltna Glacier. At that time, 1949, ski planes were being developed for landing on high altitude snow and ice.

In 1951, Bradford Washburn reached Denali's peak via the West Buttress route. In reflecting on his ascent of the mountain by that route, Washburn said:

> Denali, even by its easiest route, will never be "an easy day for a lady!" If you're reasonably experienced on high, frigid ice and rock, a good cold-weather camper, and favored by the weather gods, the West Buttress may turn out to be a fine, brief, and rewarding experience--a sort of tiny polar expedition in three dimensions. You'll also learn that what you once *did* up there won't yield half as many vivid memories as those about the wonderful

companions with whom you lived and struggled and climbed.

Washburn's West Buttress route became the standard path to the summit. It has been climbed by thousands in the years after his first ascent.

From Base Camp to the summit, the route covers a distance of 16.5 miles, and has an altitude gain of over 13,000 feet. The actual distance climbed is much greater because loads are ferried up the mountain and placed in caches, particularly above 10,000 feet. Climbers carry food and gear to a higher camp, cache the supplies in the snow, then return to sleep at the lower altitude camp. A day or two later, the climbers ascend to the cache location, and then begin this double-carry process again. This is done to lighten the loads which must be carried up the mountain and to help climbers better acclimate as they contend with the effects of higher altitudes.

As we proceeded upward, Phil pointed out the numerous cracks in the ice at the edges of the glacier. He stopped and pointed down, and told us to be careful as we stepped over a small crevasse. In awe, I looked down into the thin crack in the blue ice. Throughout the day we crossed several, and after a while, I was an old hand at striding over small crevasses.

We had been hiking steadily for about four hours, and I was beginning to tire. Basically, I felt good and was enjoying our first day of climbing on Denali, but I was ready to stop for the day when Phil announced that we had reached our first camp site. It was about 8,000 feet high, a gain of less than 1,000 feet in altitude, but we had covered nearly six miles in distance toward our goal. I was beginning to appreciate Denali's massive size.

While hiking that day, we witnessed two avalanches. The first one sounded like the firing of some distant cannon. It echoed loudly across the vast open expanse and, a second or so after we heard the blast, we saw snow burst loose and tumble down a far-off cliff face. The same thing happened later. I was awestruck by the immensity of these snow-slides. Aside from the two avalanches we saw, we heard but did not see several others. Each time, the loud distant "Boom!" captured our attention and caused us to stop walking and look around. We were glad that these avalanches were so far away, but I still wondered what Denali had in store for us.

Phil and Chris gave us instructions for setting up our tents. These are yellow and are made of a tough nylon material, and are good protection from the wind and cold. Each tent was large enough to house two of us in reasonable comfort. We were cautious in putting up the tents for it was windy. One of us held the tent fabric so that it would not blow away in the wind, with potentially serious consequences, while the other assembled the rods and placed them into the tent. After we had trampled out a flat area in the snow, we placed our tent down and secured it into the ice and snow with the metal stakes and our ice axes. Dennis and I took turns putting our sleeping bags and gear into the tent. Everything went in except our crampons, ice axes, and backpacks, which we covered in large trash bags and secured outside the tent. We placed our outer boots in the tent vestibule to keep the interior of the tent as dry as possible.

We also built snow walls around the exterior of the tents. Using snow shovels and saws that we had carried with us, we cut blocks of snow and placed them, igloo fashion, around the sides and backs of the tents to help protect them from the wind and snow.

While we stowed our gear into the tents, Chris and Phil set up the cook tent, which was a floor-less, teepee-like structure that provided some protection from the elements while we cooked and ate. When that was up, they lit a stove to begin melting snow for drinking water and cooking. This was somewhat of a long process, as the boiling of the water was hampered by the cold and altitude. When the water was ready, we each filled several of our plastic drinking bottles. Phil told us to place the bottles in between our sleeping bags in the tent at night to minimize the risk of their freezing.

I soon learned that each climber had to assist with the camp chores. This was not an opportunity to sit back, relax and be waited on by the guides. Although Phil and Chris handled the bulk of the camp responsibilities, we were all expected to help out, and Mike, Meegan, Dennis and I gladly did so. We cut blocks of snow and placed them around the tents, gathered snow in a large trash bag for melting down, collected and secured gear in the large duffel bags attached to our sleds, dug a hole in the snow into which a trash bag was placed to serve as a latrine, and did various other necessary chores. It seemed that the only task that Phil and Chris assumed without our assistance was cooking; this was something that they both seemed to enjoy.

Our spirits were generally high, although somewhat dampened by the fact that we had passed several climbers, in groups of anywhere from two to eight, who were heading down the mountain to Base Camp, turned back by the passage of time spent waiting out bad weather. All of them seemed frustrated, passing us with little more than grunting acknowledgment of our presence.

Dinner tasted great that evening. Phil had planned for us to eat the heavier items on the lower part of the mountain, so here we had cans of stew and fried chicken, while higher up we would eat our freeze dried and pre-packaged foods, so that we had lighter loads to carry. I knew that it is important to eat as much as possible so as to replace lost calories, so I ate until I could stand no more. Although I always suffer a loss of appetite at higher altitudes, it did not affect me that evening and I ate well. With each meal we had hot drinks. I had hot chocolate, which tasted particularly good in the increasingly colder weather. Mike and I gobbled up the leftovers, which became our "job" throughout the trip.

It is vital to eat and drink properly on a mountaineering expedition. A 180 pound man burns about 650 calories an hour while mountain climbing with a heavy pack. Replacing those calories requires a lot of eating. Carbohydrates are essential, followed by some proteins and a lesser amount of fats. Proper hydration is also crucial. It is recommended that an average alpine climber drink at least a gallon of fluids every day. Knowing this, I ate and drank as much as my stomach could handle every opportunity that I had.

After dinner and cleaning up of our pots and pans, we were all tired so we decided to head to bed. It felt good to climb into the sleeping bag. Mine was a brand-new bag, as yet untested, and I was anxious to see how it would perform on this trip. I was glad to snuggle up inside and found my sleeping bag to be quite warm. Dennis and I chatted for a few minutes, and then I attempted to go to sleep. I soon discovered that I had difficulty sleeping as it was not fully dark; because of our northern latitude, the sun did not completely set and it was light most of the day. I wrapped a black scarf around my eyes, and finally dozed off.

The sun is roaring, it fills to bursting each crystal of snow. I flush with feeling, moved beyond my comprehension, and once again, the warm tears freeze upon my face. These rocks and mountains, all this matter, the snow itself, the air--the earth is ringing. All is moving, full of power, full of light.

Peter Matthiessen – *The Snow Leopard*

May 22-The Beauty of the Mountain

There is no way to adequately describe the beautiful splendor of a morning such as this. The snow covered mountains around us glow in the dim morning light with a strange and sensual shimmer. "Alpenglow," it is called. I have never seen it like this, and I was glad that I had poked my head out of the tent, as I knew that moments like this are what make these trips worthwhile.

We awoke around 7:30 A.M. to the sound of Phil's call to rise. I was surprised by how well I slept, and felt relatively well rested.

I looked up at the inside of the tent, and saw it coated in a thin layer of ice. Apparently, the moisture from our respiration had condensed and frozen there. Despite our best efforts to be careful, it fell and dripped on our heads, necks and backs as we moved about, making for an uncomfortable time. I realized that this problem would persist throughout our time on Denali.

Dennis and I took turns dressing, and he had the pleasure of going first while I snuggled up for a few more minutes in the warmth of the bag. There was only room enough for one person to comfortably dress at a time, and after Dennis had finished, I took my turn. At night, I had stripped down to my long johns and a pair of down booties that I had borrowed from Mike. To put my gear on, I first climbed out of the warm sleeping bag and put on my fleece jacket and pants. Then I retrieved my two pairs of socks (liner socks and thick, wool outer socks) from the bottom of my sleeping bag where they had been put to dry while I slept. I found them surprisingly dry, as the heat from my body had done the trick. After that, I put on my boots, which was a strenuous effort because they were very cold, having spent the night in the tent vestibule, and very snug, because my feet had swollen.

Outside, the weather was warmer than it had been yesterday. As we ate our breakfast of hot oatmeal, coffee, and bagels, Phil discussed our plans for the day. We would climb to the top of Ski Hill and then, depending on the weather and how we were feeling, set up camp there. I was learning that the weather dictates all movement on McKinley, and for those poor souls who had passed us on their way back home, the weather had been their enemy. I resigned myself to the fact that I had no control over the weather, so I simply would not become overly concerned with it, and would focus instead on my own performance.

"Look," Meegan shouted, "a fox!" Sure enough, a small fox scurried across the snow field to the side of us. *What an odd sight*, I thought. Someone said "I wonder what he is doing here?" I bet the fox wondered the same thing about us.

The trip up Ski Hill was long and tedious. It was very hot, as the weather had cleared up enough so that the sun radiated off the snow. Perspiring as I pressed forward, I had some difficulty with the sled pulling me backward and sliding off to the side. Apparently the others in the group had the same problem. However, we learned to control the sleds, and the slow, steady pace that Phil had set kept us moving forward. At times, I felt as if I was back in Florida, hiking up the hill in practice for this mission, and perhaps my training in the heat helped me here.

During breaks, I could tell that Dennis was struggling. He seemed strong and was keeping up well enough, but I saw that he was suffering from pain in his lower legs. I wished that he could overcome his difficulty. Once we reached an altitude of about 9,700 feet, Phil and Chris decided that we ought to stop and camp for the night. At this height, it was windy and the temperature had dropped, which was a welcome relief from the heat we had experienced earlier in the day.

We again went through the process of establishing camp: setting up our tents and the cook tent, stowing our gear, getting the stoves burning for cooking and melting snow for water. As we gathered in the cook tent, our usual evening hangout, I felt good again, pleasantly surprised that I was doing a decent job of keeping up through our second day of climbing. It had begun snowing, and the warmth of the kitchen tent felt good as we huddled inside to enjoy dinner. Ellen and Romulo had set up camp next to us, and they joined us for dinner. We all seemed in good spirits and enjoyed a lively conversation.

After dinner, we had some soup left over and, noticing that a small group was camped nearby, Meegan volunteered to carry it over to them. When she came back, she said that one of the climbers had no legs. His name was Ed Hommer.

Hommer was an Alaskan bush pilot who had crashed his plane on Mount McKinley in 1981. He and his three passengers were trapped in the aircraft during a five-day winter storm. Two of the passengers died before Ed and the surviving passenger were miraculously rescued. As a result, Ed lost both of his lower legs to frostbite. Years later, his legs were fitted with special state-of-the-art prosthetic devices. When he told her that, Meegan did not believe that his legs were artificial. To prove it, he loudly slammed his metal ice axe against his lower legs, conclusively demonstrating that they were metal.

After suffering years of depression and alcoholism while recovering from his physical injuries, Hommer decided to change his life around. Together with his climbing partner, he returned to conquer the mountain on which he had nearly perished. A reporter from the Dateline television program was with him, and the producers had given Ed and his partner a camera and tripod to film their expedition. Meegan wished them success.

We enjoyed Meegan's report, shared some jokes, and discussed more serious issues. Our group seemed to be interacting very well. I realized that it was early in the expedition and that we were all on our best behavior, and that our levels of irritability would rise as time passed, but it appeared that we were a good mix and we enjoyed each other's company. Chris, Mike and Meegan, being close in age, got along very well together, and acted as if they had known each other for more than a few days. Dennis and I were close, and the rigors of the climb had not dampened our friendship. Phil seemed pleased with our growing companionship, and told us that we had all done a great job so far. I felt that I was performing well physically and my level of energy was high. I was concerned about Dennis, though, as he continued to have pain in his lower legs.

There have been joys too great to be described in words, and there have been griefs upon which I have dared not to dwell; and with these in mind I say: Climb if you will, but remember that courage and strength are naught without prudence, and that a momentary negligence may destroy the happiness of a lifetime. Do nothing in haste; look well to each step, and from the beginning think what may be the end.

Edward Whymper – *Scrambles Amongst the Alps*

May 23-Sitting Out a Snowstorm

Poor weather greeted us as we arose from our slumber. It was cold, windy and snowing. During the night, sleep was difficult because of the racket caused by the wind, which rattled the fabric of the tent so that it sounded like a machine gun. I would experience that racket throughout our expedition, but eventually grew used to it.

Snow had covered our tent and Dennis and I had to shake it off from inside. We got up for breakfast, and found that it had snowed about twelve inches. Our plan was to carry gear and supplies up to 11,000 feet today, but when Phil assessed the weather conditions, he announced that we had better stay put until it improved.

The general theory for climbing Denali is to move in poor weather on the lower part of the mountain, if it is not too bad, but to wait for good weather to proceed on the upper part. However, we were now experiencing nearly whiteout conditions, and it looked too dangerous to go anywhere, so we stayed put. After breakfast, we helped clear snow from our camp area using the snow shovels and our feet to stomp it down. We saw some other climbers slowly moving up the mountain past our camp site. "Hardy souls," I thought, appreciating the fact that we were staying in camp as I saw them struggle against the blustery snow and wind.

There was not much else to do, so we went back to our tents to wait out the weather. At first, it felt great to return to the warmth of my sleeping bag. Dennis and I talked for a while, then read and listened to our tiny radios, which were hard to hear because of the static. Dennis explained that as we got higher up the mountain where the signals would not be blocked by the surrounding rock walls, our radio reception would improve. Thus, we passed time this way, occasionally leaving the tent to attend to bodily functions, to dig snow that had accumulated around our tents, or to visit the cook tent. It was snowing like crazy, and I was surprised by how rapidly it accumulated. Condemned to our tents for the day, all of us were bored stiff.

Going to the bathroom is a huge problem. To go out of the tent, one must bundle up. If you stay out too long "taking care of business," exposed body parts become numb from the cold and lose all feeling. Imagine what it is like to use frozen fingers to wipe a numb backside. I promise you, it is no fun.

Built about twenty feet from the tents, our latrines on Denali consisted of a trash bag-lined hole in the snow. Walls built of snow blocks provided a modicum of privacy. When we moved our camp, we took the bag, sealed it, and threw it into a designated large crevasse. Since it is difficult to get up and dress to go out of the tent to urinate at night, we resorted to using "pee-bottles" for that purpose. For the males, this process is easy. Although I have no personal knowledge, I understood that the females had to use a type of funnel when using the pee-bottles. Of course, those bottles were clearly marked so that we did not confuse them with the drinking water.

Dennis had a thermometer, and checked the temperature inside the tent each night. As I curled up in my warm bag, he told me that it was twenty below zero. I knew it was awfully cold, but had no idea it was that bad. That was the last time that he looked at that thermometer.

Great things are done when men and mountains meet; This is not done by jostling in the street.

William Blake – *Gnomic Verses*

May 24-Fried by the Sun

The weather had improved by the next morning. It stopped snowing and warmed considerably. Phil announced that we would make a carry of gear up to about 11,000 feet, and, after a breakfast of Cheerios, bagels, and coffee, we happily set out. Since the weather was warmer, we were comfortable wearing only long johns while we hiked, although it was cold when we stopped for breaks. Remembering what Dennis had told me about "never being so hot, and never being so cold," I was again experiencing the hot part. I was sweating profusely, which annoyingly caused the sun screen to drip down my face into my eyes and mouth.

We all laughed at Mike. He had cut up the empty Cheerios box and, using part of the cut-out cardboard, fashioned a shield for his nose by attaching it to his sunglasses. Although it might have been effective for a while, it continued to slip down and didn't last long.

During breaks, we drank water, snacked on salami, cheese, crackers and candy, replenished sun screen, and put sun block on our lips. Our exposed skin, particularly on our faces and hands, became chapped and sunburned quickly in the dry, cold and windy environment. The worst spot was always the bottom of our noses. Snot constantly ran from our noses, and the reflection of the sun from the glacial ice and snow magnified upward onto that exposed area. The bottom of my nose was constantly red and sore.

Despite all precautions, our faces continued to be reddened by the wind, cold and sun. We wore dark sunglasses or ski goggles all the time on the mountain, whether it was cloudy or clear. Ultraviolet radiation levels increase with altitude, and at heights above 13,000 feet, it can result in serious damage to the eyes. Our glasses and goggles did a great job of protecting our eyes from the effects of the sun reflecting off the brilliantly white snow, but we all wound up with a case of "raccoon eyes," with the protected white skin around our eyes striking out in stark contrast to the red sunburned skin of our faces.

Sitting on my pack while enjoying our respite, I nearly broke a tooth when I bit down hard on my frozen candy bar. I should have known better. This was a continual problem throughout the expedition-trying to keep candies in a place where they would not freeze or melt inside my pack.

As we approached 11,000 feet, the scenery was spectacular. Nearby, sharp cliffs and snow-covered mountain peaks glowed brilliantly in the sunshine. Lush green of the distant flat, forested lands spread out below. What a remarkably magnificent place.

I noticed that it had also grown progressively colder, and the wind had increased. We soon had to put on heavier clothing to stay warm. We stopped and placed a cache in an open area that was free of crevasses, placing food and other gear into a couple of large duffel bags, then burying them in the snow. We then placed a few bamboo wands with small flags on them into the snow to mark our cache. We asked Phil if anyone would steal our goods. "No," he said, "climbers mind their own business, and this won't be disturbed unless it's an emergency." After securing the cache, we began the hike back down to our camp at 9,000 feet to spend the night there, hoping to return up here the next day. The climb down, without heavy loads, was easy and it felt good to travel at a quicker pace.

Mountains are not fair or unfair, they are just dangerous.

Reinhold Messner – *All Fourteen 8000ers*

May 25-Denali Turns Deadly

We were greeted by a steady snowfall and brisk winds as we arose. Judging from the accumulation, it must have snowed all night. Phil assessed the weather, and told us that we would have to sit out the storm before moving. Waiting out the weather seemed to affect the morale of everyone in our group. We were anxious to move up the mountain, and it seemed as if each day detained at this relatively low altitude was truly useless. We again occupied ourselves by clearing snow around our tents and camp site, eating, conversing, reading and listening to radios. I spent a large part of my time in the comfort of my cocoon, wrapped tightly inside my sleeping bag, dropping in and out of sleep as the hours dragged on.

We heard from some climbers descending the mountain that search parties were attempting to locate some missing climbers. They said that a Canadian climber had slipped and fallen from the ridge line near the 16,000 foot level, and a ranger, who was on the ridge near him, went to search for the fallen climber. Both the climber and the ranger had disappeared.

Yesterday, when the weather was not storming, we heard helicopters far above us on the mountain. It was almost constant, the sound of choppers too distant to see. Phil told us that they were probably searching for missing climbers. We felt starved for information, and eagerly approached those descending climbers who paused to speak with us, gleaning bits of knowledge from each. However, from speaking with them, we learned little more than what we already knew.

As we gathered for dinner in the cook tent, the mood was comparatively somber. The snow continued, but it did appear as if it was starting to clear. "It sure takes a lot of patience to climb this mountain," I announced, rather philosophically. Phil said, "That's right," looking at me as if I had come to some significant revelation. The others nodded in assent. Although not very profound, I knew that was really a true statement, and if I could avoid becoming impatient, it would help.

After we had eaten, we bagged up our trash. As most of the commercial guides do, Phil encouraged us to practice "clean climbing." This meant that we did not leave any trash or debris on the mountain. Our empty gas cans, boxes, paper wrappers, everything was bagged up and carried back off the mountain. Our poop was bagged and deposited into nearby large crevasses, to be ground into bits by the constantly moving glaciers. Rarely did we encounter other climbers' garbage on the mountain, but if we did, we picked it up and carried it with us.

Although he had maintained communication at the beginning of the expedition, Mike tried several times to contact his class with his satellite phone, but it was not working properly. He was extremely disappointed that he could not communicate with his students and knew that they would be very concerned and worried when they hadn't heard from him. He also had a cell phone, and he decided to call them once we got higher up the mountain where it might transmit without interference from the surrounding mountain walls.

Climbing is the lazy man's way to enlightenment. It forces you to pay attention, because if you don't, you won't succeed, which is minor--or you may get hurt, which is major. Instead of years of meditation, you have this activity that forces you to relax and monitor your breathing and tread the line between living and dying. When you climb, you always are confronted with the edge. Hey, if it was just like climbing a ladder, we would have quit a long time ago.

Duncan Ferguson

May 26-Climbing into a Whiteout

I have never seen so much snow. As a child growing up in New Jersey, we had snowstorms and I have witnessed some deep snow, but that was nothing compared to this. It was unbelievable how much it had snowed during the past day and night. The door of our tent was nearly covered and we spent a considerable amount of time digging the tents out.

It was very cloudy, the sky was leaden and hazy, and visibility was extremely poor. The wind was blowing very strongly, making it difficult to walk about, but it was not snowing, so we decided to pack up and go.

We were glad to start moving from the 9,000 foot camp even though the snow was deep, which made travel very slow and difficult. Phil, using skis, was in the lead, and I was on the rope behind him, plodding along in snowshoes. Mike was behind me, then Meegan, Dennis and Chris, which was our usual lineup. Chris, like Phil, wore skis, while the others wore snowshoes. We were having a difficult time, as even with the assistance of the skis and snowshoes, we sank into the deep snow with each step that we took. Often, I dropped all the way down until the snow was over my knees. Walking was exhausting work. I thought that those behind me had a slightly easier time of it because Phil and I were clearing the way, but when I looked back, I saw that they were struggling as well.

Then it began to snow. Between the snow, wind and clouds, visibility became increasingly worse. It reached the point where we could barely see the person in front or in back of us. Although it was not a blizzard, the wind was whipping up the snow in blinding sheets. We were experiencing a white-out. If any climbers had preceded us, their trail had been quickly covered over by the drifting snow. Phil told us that had we been higher up on the mountain, we would not be moving under these conditions. He focused all of his attention on route finding. Other climbing parties had placed bamboo wands along the route, each wand having a small colored strip of material attached. As we proceeded slowly along, we all joined in searching for these wands.

Hiking in these conditions reminded me of my first climb on Mt. Rainier several years before this expedition. As a first-time climber, I was obviously very nervous. It was a large group of mostly novice climbers, and Phil led the climb, assisted by several junior guides. We packed up our gear, put on our backpacks and left the hut at Paradise, where the parking lot, hotel and facilities are located. We began climbing up the Muir snowfield, a long, upward sloping incline. Although the weather was fairly good at the start, it got progressively worse. Eventually, we were in a full-blown snowstorm. It was overcast, windy, snowing and cold. Our group had spread out, some faster ones with Phil up ahead, and some slower ones with assistant guides behind. I was about in the middle.

The guides began shouting at us to put our crampons on. Before this, I had no training or experience with crampons. As a matter of fact, I had no idea of how to put them on. I sat down on my pack, and a guide came along to assist me. Clumsily, with freezing fingers, I worked the straps around my feet and ankles, and eventually got the crampons secured to my boots. By then, the visibility was horrible.

I stood up, and saw no one in front of me. I looked back, and saw no one there either. I decided to go forward, and anxiously rambled onward as fast as I could go. After what seemed like an eternity, I spotted someone ahead of me. I quickened my pace and caught up, recognizing it as one of the climbers in our group. Soon, the slope steepened and I saw above me our destination for the day, the hut at Camp Muir.

Breathing heavily from the physical effort and nervousness, as I approached the hut, I saw Phil standing at the door. I looked at him as I entered, and saw long icicles dangling from his mustache. I was never so happy to see a frozen face.

As we continued our ascent of Denali, Phil had a G.P.S. device, and he often stopped to use it to orient ourselves. We then set off again in the right direction. Once, when we stopped to search for a wand, we spotted something dark in the snow ahead of us. Thinking it was a wand, we approached only to find a small gray bird lying dead in the snow. Apparently, it had frozen to death. We saw several more of these unfortunate creatures during the day, causing Meegan to wonder aloud, "It's hard to believe that these birds would be here even in good weather."

Later in the day, the white-out conditions improved, the wind subsided and the skies cleared, and we found the going much better. As we took one of our breaks, Phil complimented us on how well we had done under difficult conditions. Not only was the climbing physically demanding because of the deep snow, it was difficult because of the poor visibility. There were times during the day when I wondered if we would be lost. Several times Phil had stopped and conferred with Chris outside of our hearing, and they appeared clearly concerned. *What if we had wandered off track and gotten lost? What if we meandered into a crevasse?* Although I had these frightening thoughts, I had great confidence in Phil and Chris. I wouldn't have chosen anyone else to lead us, at that time or at any other during our expedition.

Other climbers passed us as they descended. We overheard one of the guides talking with Phil. He said that one group had spent seven days at a camp at 11,000 feet and then given up, returning to the Base Camp to go home. Obviously, that was very disturbing news for us.

Most of the day our route had risen gradually, but as we approached 11,000 feet, it inclined abruptly. Although the climbing became more difficult, we were rewarded with spectacular views. The weather had cleared, and we arrived at the relatively flat area where we had previously placed our cache. To our left rose the bulk of Denali's West Buttress and, hidden from view, the summit. To the right, the mountain dropped off, with white clouds streaming in the invisible wind below. Further off, we saw the flat, open Alaskan countryside we had flown over on our way to Denali, with a narrow ribbon of a river winding its way through the forested lands before disappearing in the distance. Mike and I took out our cameras and snapped photographs. I was so enthralled with the view that I had not noticed that the rest of the group was busy setting up camp.

We placed our tents near the trail by our cache. When we finished setting up camp, I felt hungry and exhausted. Chris set up the stove and soon had a pot of boiling water ready. As usual, the first order of business was a cup of hot soup. After that we enjoyed a hearty meal and hot drinks. We all ate until we were stuffed and, since there were some leftovers, Chris encouraged us to finish it up. As usual, Mike and I were the only takers. After a difficult day, it felt good to climb into the tent for the evening. If the weather permitted, we would carry a load of supplies to cache higher up the mountain, perhaps up to 14,000 feet. While we ate, we discussed the fact that many climbers had left the higher camps to return to the Base Camp. How depressing it must be, we agreed, to reach that altitude only to be turned back by bad weather.

As we turned in for the night, we again heard the sound of helicopters flying above us. Apparently, the search for the missing Canadian climber and the ranger was continuing. It was unsettling to hear this, but we were all well aware of the risks and did not dwell on thoughts of our own possible misfortunes.

Many months after our expedition, sitting in an easy chair in the comfort of my home, I learned what had happened. Deteriorating weather conditions had forced two Canadian climbers to abandon their summit attempt and descend from the 17,200-foot High Camp on May 24. Mike Vanderbeek and Tim Hurtado, two National Park Service volunteer patrol members, who are called "rangers," were also at the High Camp. They descended on the same route shortly after the Canadian pair, and soon overtook them. Winds were steady at 30 mph, with gusts up to 60-70 mph, so they proceeded carefully. The rangers stopped from time to time to keep an eye on the Canadian climbers.

On a steep section of the ridgeline, one of the Canadian climbers slipped and fell. The rangers were about 100 feet further down the route, and were able to see the fallen climber 50 feet below the ridge crest, catapulting downward. The rangers radioed for assistance, and then went to the aid of the fallen Canadian climber.

Climbing down from the ridgeline, the rangers descended the steepening wall, encountering sections of hard ice in the process. They spotted patches of blood, and followed those downward. The rangers were not roped together. Realizing that he was in a predicament, having reached a huge section of steep, hard blue ice, with difficult footing and poor visibility, Tim Hurtado stopped and anchored himself to the wall. He maintained voice contact with the other ranger, Mike Vanderbeek, but soon heard the sound of "nylon on ice," after which he lost contact with Vandeerbeek. Mike Vanderbeek had also fallen.

Over the next four days, a major rescue effort ensued. Extreme weather hampered attempts for the first few days, and then it cleared. The Canadian climber's body was recovered. Although they found his pack and many of his personal items, Mike Vanderbeek's body was not located and was presumed lost in the bergschrund or a crevasse on the Peters Glacier far below.

As we sat in our tent, I looked over at Dennis and saw that he was in pain. Dennis had been really struggling over the past two days. He had purchased new boots for this trip, and they continued to cut into his ankles, which were now painfully raw and bleeding. His situation had not improved today, and he told me that he was considering turning back. Dennis had a long talk with Phil and weighed his options. Since he was in obvious pain, and saw no hope of improvement, Dennis made the extremely difficult decision to return home.

Chris volunteered to hike back down to Base Camp with Dennis, together with a climber from an RMI party who was also having difficulty. They would leave in the morning. Dennis and I discussed his leaving, and it was distressing for both of us. We had gotten to know each other very well, and had become good friends. Part of the joy of mountain climbing is the friendships that one develops, and Dennis was a true example of that. Undoubtedly, I would miss his company very much.

Since he was returning to civilization, Dennis offered to take messages back home for us. Mike wanted Dennis to contact his students and tell them that the satellite phone was not operating properly, that everything was alright, and that he would try to contact them by cell phone once we were higher up the mountain. We all had messages for our families, telling them that we missed them, that they were in our thoughts constantly, and that we loved them very much.

That night I had a strange dream. I dreamt that I had gone home from the mountain to spend the night there. In my dream, I was extremely anxious because I wanted to stay home, but I had to return to Denali early the next morning. Actually, this was the third night in a row that I had a dream similar to this one. Each time, I dreamt that I had gone home and worried about having to get back to the expedition. I dreamt of spending time at home with my family, but was consumed with anxiety about returning to my group on the mountain. Each dream was as vivid as real life. I woke up very distressed. I do not know whether it was the effects of our physical exertion or the increased altitude, but I truly felt that I was losing my mind. I told no one in my party about these dreams for fear that they would think my sanity had abandoned me. After the expedition, I learned that these dreams are not uncommon, and are probably the result of a high level of anxiety mixed with a low dose of oxygen.

Eastward the dawn rose, ridge behind ridge into the morning, and vanished out of eyesight into guess; it was no more than a glimmer blending with the hem of the sky, but it spoke to them, out of memory and old tales, of the high and distant mountains.

J.R.R. Tolkien – *The Lord of the Rings*

May 27-A Very Windy Corner

Again, there was a heavy snowfall last night, but the weather looked pretty good. As we ate breakfast this morning, we talked with Dennis about his impending departure. Although he was very disappointed to have to turn back on what was likely his last attempt at Denali, Dennis seemed to be relieved by the certainty of his decision to abandon the attempt. I am sure that he wondered whether he could have continued the expedition, and how the disability of his lacerated ankles may have impacted the rest of the group. In any event, his internal struggle had ended and it appeared that a burden had lifted from him, and I knew that he had made the right decision. Still, I was sad to see him go.

As Chris and Dennis prepared to descend, we packed our gear for a carry up to 14,000 feet. After breakfast, we bid our final farewells to Dennis. It was heartbreaking to watch Dennis and Chris gradually fade in the distance as they marched downward, following our ascending footprints. In a way, though, I envied Dennis, because soon he would be returning to the comforts of home. We all dearly missed the typical substances of our daily lives we too often take for granted: hot showers, warm beds, cold beer, decent meals, and the companionship of friends and family.

As we considered our plan for the day, I reflected on how I was doing so far. It was gratifying to realize that I was keeping up with the group and actually felt as if I was performing better than I anticipated. So far, so good.

We packed up the gear that we would carry to the higher cache, which included food, fuel, and other items no longer needed at the lower camp. Lugging gear to leave in a cache was necessary but unsatisfying work. There was simply too much weight to carry safely on the steeper slopes we would encounter higher up on the mountain. We really had no other choice but to haul equipment up there and leave it until we were able to move up to retrieve it.

Romulo and Ellen joined us. Since Chris was not there to assist Phil, they agreed to follow our rope team, which was now short two climbers. It was good to have their company.

The route commenced with a climb up the steep Motorcycle Hill. The sun was shining and the weather was very good, and it actually became awfully warm as we ascended the sharp incline. For our efforts, we were rewarded with stunning views from the top of the hill. We continued on in our typical expedition fashion, proceeding slowly and meticulously, one step after another, taking short breaks for snacks and drinks every hour or so. After topping the hill, we crossed a broad plateau approaching the section of Denali known as Windy Corner.

Aptly named Windy Corner is the point at the top of the plateau where the route turns abruptly around a corner created by the West Buttress, which rises sharply above. Winds are ferocious on this part of the mountain. Chris and Phil had warned us about Windy Corner, telling us that it was rarely without strong winds. When we ascended Motorcycle Hill and the plateau above it, we had gotten warm and stripped down to cool off. I was unaware that we were approaching Windy Corner. As we did, the winds were blowing and gusting, and it became incredibly cold. The snow underfoot had given way to blue ice, probably as a result of the incessant winds. We continued to move up slowly. As we did, we were pelted by hard bits of ice which were being shot across the slick slope by the wind. They stung as they hit my face, and it felt like bees were stinging me. The pain was intensified by the fierce cold. As the body struggles to maintain warmth in cold temperatures, blood is sacrificed from the extremities to keep the body's core--the brain, heart and lungs--at a normal temperature. Thus, fingers, toes, ears and noses freeze first, and mine were getting mighty cold. While we had been rather warm a few moments earlier, now the force of the cold wind made us shiver, and we struggled to zip up jackets that were open and to pull hoods and hats over our heads.

We surmounted Windy Corner and, since we had been climbing for most of the day and the group was tired, Phil elected to put our cache in at an altitude of 13,500 feet rather than to continue to push up to the camp at 14,200. Actually, it is not unusual to do that, as the 13,500 foot area provides a relatively safe and secure location. There were several other caches made there. We placed our duffel bags in an abandoned cache after first digging it out with our snow shovels.

As we worked on placing our cache, I noticed that there was a tent set up nearby. After a while, two climbers emerged. They looked disheveled and dispirited. The climbers came over and spoke with us, explaining that they were Canadian, and that one of them had fallen into a crevasse just above this camp site. Although he was extracted from the crevasse without injury, the pair had lost some essential equipment, including their stove and a sleeping bag. Unfortunately for them, their trip was over as they had to abandon their effort to scale McKinley. They were simply trying to muster the energy for a voyage back to Base Camp. There was nothing we could do for them, and we bid them good luck.

Until we got higher up on the steeper part of the mountain, crevasses were a major concern. I recalled all too well reading about a deadly crevasse incident on Denali involving the renowned mountaineer, Jim Wickwire. An attorney from the State of Washington, Jim pursued an active and successful climbing career. In 1978, he became the first American to summit K2. Located in Pakistan, K2 is known as the "Savage

Mountain" because of the difficulty of the ascent and its high fatality rate. On the descent, he was forced to take emergency shelter at an altitude of 27,750 feet, spending a bitterly cold night in a nylon bivouac sack. Although debilitated and miserable, he miraculously survived.

To prepare for an expedition to Mt. Everest in 1981, Wickwire went to climb Denali with Chris Kerrebrock, a 25-year old guide on Mt. Rainier. Taking a different and more difficult route than the one that we were on, they were roped together with a sled carrying supplies tied between them, crossing the Peters Glacier. Glaciers appear flat and solid, but they are actually rippled and moving. The surface of the glacier will often rupture, creating a crack that can sometimes be hundreds of feet deep. Called crevasses, these fissures vary in width from a few inches to up to 65 feet. Often they are visible and easy to avoid. However, they are sometimes undetectable, hidden by snow or ice.

As they crossed the Peters Glacier, Chris Kerrebrock suddenly toppled head first into an unseen crevasse. The sled behind him snapped into the gap behind him. Knocked off his feet, Jim Wickwire was also suddenly yanked into the crevasse. Chris was upside down, his body and heavy pack wedged between the walls of the crevasse, with the sled and Jim on top of him. It was impossible for Chris to move.

Jim had broken a shoulder in the fall. With movement limited by the cramped space, Jim was able to dislodge the sled from on top of Chris, took off his snowshoes and put on his crampons. He realized that he had to extradite himself from the trap so that he could try to rescue Chris. Chipping indentations into the icy wall and using the points of his crampons, Wickwire was able to slowly climb out of the crevasse. In the meantime, Chris remained entombed in the crevasse, calling out for help.

Jim spent hours and tried everything in his power to rescue Chris, but could not get him out. His attempts to radio for help were futile, because they were in such an isolated location. Finally, realizing that he could do no more and conceding that rescue was impossible, he stayed by the crevasse, where Chris slowly perished. Chris, an avid trumpet player, asked Jim to place the mouthpiece of his trumpet on the summit of Mt. Everest. Wickwire promised that if he did not do it, someone else would. Shivering in a nylon bivouac bag on the glacier, injured and racked with guilt and remorse, Jim heard Chris singing songs as he slowly passed away. Demonstrating the difficulty of the jam that Chris Kerrebrock was in, it took several rangers an entire day, chipping away at ice and using pulleys, to remove Chris's body from its icy grave. A few years afterwards, Phil Ershler carried through on Wickwire's promise and buried Chris Kerrebrock's trumpet mouthpiece on the summit of Mt. Everest.

Although Mike and Meegan seemed to share my feeling of sadness for the Canadian climbers we had just met, the Denali veterans, Phil and Chris, didn't have much sympathy. This was something that I had observed throughout the expedition; while we clients were often concerned for the plight of other climbers, whether it be these guys or those many poor souls that had passed us descending the mountain because they were turned back by the weather, Phil, Chris, and the other guides we encountered took a more detached and matter of fact approach. They asked question to learn as much information as they could about the trail or weather conditions, but did not become emotionally involved. I began to understand that they had to maintain this detached attitude during expeditions. Clearly, they had us and themselves to be concerned about, and could not be distracted by the difficulties of others.

Regardless of their unemotional attitudes, the guides were quick to assist others who were in trouble. This was expected as general mountaineering protocol. If other climbers are in danger, the guides will readily jump to assist, regardless of whether it is a minor injury or a major search and rescue. Further, if there is trouble, we clients may have to help. This mountaineering etiquette is true on all mountains, not just on Denali.

Our return to our camp at 11,000 feet was uneventful. Again, I was exhausted after a long day, and fell into a deep sleep.

Hours slide by like minutes. The accumulated clutter of day-to-day existence--the lapses of conscience, the unpaid bills, the bungled opportunities, the dust under the couch, the inescapable prison of your genes-- all of it is temporarily forgotten, crowded from your thoughts by an overpowering clarity of purpose by the seriousness of the task at hand.

Jon Krakauer – *Into the Wild*

May 28-Alone in a Tent

I awoke again to awful weather. It was very cold and snowing to the point that visibility was limited to a few feet. As usual, I slowly emerged from the warmth of the sleeping bag, reluctant to stir, but anxious to see what the mountain had in store for us today. I heard voices from the other tents, and we soon began discussing the weather. Phil, as usual, was cautiously optimistic, and advised that we would sit tight to see how the weather turned out.

Last night was the first that I spent alone in the tent. I considered Dennis' leaving with mixed feelings; on one hand, I would miss him badly, but on the other, I would enjoy the extra room in the cramped tent. However, even though I had more space, it was remarkably colder without another body in the tent, and I had difficulty sleeping because of that. It just was not the same, waking up without Dennis there to greet me.

Although there are planned rest days during the trip, they were not anticipated until higher up on the mountain. We were now on our third day of inactivity, all on account of the poor weather. We still had plenty of time, but it was disconcerting to know that we had lost three days of climbing due to poor weather.

We spent this day much the same as the others, reading and sleeping in our tents, and enjoying our meals together in the cook tent. The mood of the group was somewhat dismal, considering that the weather had been so uncooperative. Hopefully, we would move up the mountain tomorrow.

There is no hill that never ends.

Maasai proverb

May 29-The Basin Camp

ood news greeted us as we arose. Phil announced that the storm had passed and that we were ascending to the 14,000-foot camp. We quickly assembled in the cook tent for breakfast, and Phil gave us our instructions, telling us that we would pack up as soon as possible then proceed up to set up camp. We would then return to retrieve our cache of supplies which we had placed at 13,500 feet a couple of days ago.

The Basin Camp is a milestone. Located at 14,200 feet, it is situated on a huge plateau protected in part from the weather by the immense steep wall of the West Buttress. It is called the Basin Camp because it appears to be one-half of a huge bowl, with the wall of the West Buttress rising nearly 2,000 feet above. Across the plateau from the wall, the flat plain drops sharply. The lip of the plateau at this drop-off point is called the Edge of the World, and the mountain plummets several thousand feet here. I remember Dennis telling me about this spot, and showing me a photograph of him sitting on a rock, an apparent plunge in the earth below him, with a panoramic vista of snow covered mountains in the background. When I saw that photograph, I wondered if I would ever reach that spot. Hopefully, I would today.

With Dennis and Chris both gone, we roped up with Phil in the lead ahead of me, Meegan behind me, and Mike at the end. We set off at our usual slow and deliberate pace, one step, a deep breath, and then another step. We retraced the route that we had taken two days ago, but this time the climbing seemed easier. As usual, we hiked for about an hour, and then took a break for a drink of water and a snack.

A major difference between this expedition and others I have taken was that Phil now gave us minimal instructions. On my earlier expeditions, he instructed us on how to use the "rest-step," locking the knee to briefly rest the leg while the other foot steps up, so as to take the pressure off the muscles and put it on the bones; how to "pressure-breathe," deeply sucking air into the lungs so as to maximize oxygen intake, while forcefully blowing the air out when exhaling, thereby increasing the pressure in the lungs; how to hydrate properly by drinking water profusely at each break; and how to take in as many calories as possible by eating on breaks. On prior trips, Phil had carefully demonstrated proper rope, crampon and ice axe techniques. I understood that on Denali, however, such instructions were unnecessary. This was not a training expedition. Phil knew each of us and our climbing abilities, and he trusted that we had the basic skills needed for a Denali expedition.

After hours of climbing, we reached the location of our cache. We took a break, then, using the snow shovels, dug open the icy cache to remove some items to carry up with us, and we opened our frozen duffel bags to remove some gear that we would leave in that spot, primarily food for the trip back down. I noticed that the snowfall had buried a large part of the bamboo marker, and worried about how we could locate our gear on the way down if a huge snowstorm ensued.

Although tired from the effort needed to reach this point, we were enthusiastic as we set off for the Basin Camp, which was only about 700 feet above. The route continued to moderately rise, but it seemed as if the camp would never come into sight. In climbing, as in other facets of life, the closer one gets to the goal, the more slowly it seems to approach. Finally, I spotted tents in the distance. I was exhausted, and it felt like my load had doubled in weight, but I was happy to realize that we had arrived.

Phil led us through the middle of the camp, which consisted of approximately 25 tents of various colors spread out across the flat plateau. The route was rutted by tracks crisscrossing through the snow, which added to the difficulty of dragging the sleds behind us. As if we were aliens entering a strange land, we passed through this multi-colored tent city. The occupants stood outside, studying us with detached interest.

We decided to stay at the far edge of the encampment, nearer to the Headwall of the West Buttress. Since it was late in the day and we had much to do, Phil prompted us to unpack our tents and get camp set up. I was distracted by my surroundings, and kept looking around in amazement. Spread out before me were the camps of climbers from all around the world. All of the tents were surrounded by blocks of snow formed into walls. Each had a cache situated nearby. Colorful clothing was hung along the tents and snow walls. Climbers milled about in various stages of activity.

Many of them had their attention focused on a spot high above us. We looked up and saw what had captured their attention. Up above and far to the right of the Headwall, two small, dark dots were barely visible against the stark white background of the mountainside. We learned that two climbers had attempted to descend from the High Camp, located just out of sight over the crest of the high ridge. They were climbing down a narrow gap called "Rescue Gully," which ran down the precipitous face of the snow and ice wall. It is a steep and dangerous shortcut from the High Camp at 17,000 feet to the Basin Camp where we were. Apparently, one of the climbers had fallen into a crevasse coming down Rescue Gully, and the other had slowly worked his way down to pull the fallen climber out. He must have been successful, because there were two of them next to the crevasse, which appeared as a small, dark, narrow gap across the face of the cliff. Throughout the day, they entertained the spectators below, who were enthralled and quite delighted to follow the climbers' slow and deliberate progress down the steep wall. From that distance, they appeared as if they were two black ants engaged in a slow motion dance.

Beyond the tents and sitting alone in a vast open area in the middle of the Basin Camp was the latrine--a wooden seat with bamboo markers around it. There were several people in line, politely standing a few feet from the structure while it was being used by a climber. There was absolutely no privacy, but what a view. From the seat on the "throne," one could look out at Mt. Foraker rising majestically in the foreground, with the vast and beautiful Alaskan mountain range spread out behind. Not being one to pass up a restroom when I see one, I jumped in line. It was a bit bizarre, going to the bathroom while others stood behind me, but they were politely looking off at the beautiful scenery rather than watching my cold bare butt.

To the left of and a distance away from the latrine were two large tents, one red and one yellow. One tent houses a medical station, and the other is the home of the Denali National Park mountain rangers.

Headquartered in Talkeetna, the mountain rangers patrol Denali, Mt. Hunter, and the other mountains located in the area of Denali National Park. A ranger will be stationed at the Denali Base Camp, and another at the Basin Camp, each for about a thirty-day stint. Assisted by roughly six volunteers, including doctors and experienced mountaineers, the rangers will patrol the mountain, educating and assisting climbers, cleaning up trash, and maintaining the latrine. Perhaps they are best known for their search and rescue operations. The rangers and volunteers are hardy individuals, who prove an invaluable service for climbers. There is a great deal of competition to become a Denali ranger or volunteer. These are coveted positions, and the rangers work hard in harsh and dangerous conditions. They deserve every bit of the honor and respect that they receive.

The other tent houses the medical station for the rangers. There, they can provide emergency medical attention for injured or ill climbers. I understood that having medical facilities and rangers on the mountain was a double-edged sword. On one hand, it was great to have needed assistance for missing or injured climbers. On the other hand, however, many inexperienced or careless climbers found their way onto the flanks of Denali, and there are too many stories of those climbers being rescued by rangers or receiving medical attention for issues caused by their own negligence. Thus, some have complained that these facilities have reduced climbers' self-reliance and sufficiency.

We spent the remainder of the day setting up our tents, building snow walls around them, and cooking our dinner. I felt the influence of the increased altitude, and had greater difficulty breathing than I had so far. It was an effort to take in enough oxygen, and I often felt like I was sucking air through a straw.

Mike attempted many times over the past several days to contact his class by the satellite phone, without success. The phone could not transmit signals from most of the areas on the mountain. Unbeknownst to us, the students were worried since they hadn't heard from Mike since May 25, so they put out a call for information on their website.

Phil explained that we would spend the day here tomorrow, except for a trip back to our cache at 13,500 feet to retrieve some of the gear we had left behind yesterday. If the weather permitted, perhaps we would carry some gear up to the High Camp at 17,000 feet.

That meant climbing the Headwall. I had heard much about the Headwall. When I had spoken with others who had climbed the wall, their eyes widened as they sought vainly to express the awe the Headwall inspired. And now, here I was.

To say that the Headwall looked intimidating is an understatement. Most climbers in camp were, like me, silently staring up at it as if entranced by some mysterious monolith.

The steepest climbing of the entire route lies above the Basin Camp. From the Basin Camp at 14,200 feet, the route ascends to a height of 16,200 feet at the top of the West Buttress ridge. The Headwall leads to the top of the ridge. It is an 800 foot, 40-55 degree, snow and ice wall. The steeper sections of it are secured by ropes permanently fixed into the mountainside. Since it is too steep to carry sleds up the Headwall, and too difficult to bring very heavy loads, we would have to make at least two trips up and down, one to carry and leave gear at the High Camp, and the other when we went up for our summit attempt. Before we arrived, I had agonized over my ability to handle this steep and exposed climbing. Now as I stood behind my tent and looked up at the wall, I had a knot in my stomach.

As I sat in my tent, I wondered whether I had made a mistake in coming here, that maybe I was in over my head. As much as I did not want to let myself down, I did not want to disappoint Phil and the members of my group. On top of the physical difficulty of surviving in this cold and altitude, I let my anxieties get the best of me.

I climbed into my sleeping bag early, and tried to distract myself by reading the suspense novel that I had brought along, but I could not stop myself from unzipping the door of my tent and peering out into the luminescent Alaskan night, again wondering why I was here.

When you ride your bike, you're working your legs, but your mind is on a treadmill. When you play chess, your mind is clicking along, but your body is stagnating. Climbing brings it together in a beautiful, magical way. The adrenaline is flowing, and it's flowing all the time.

Pat Ament

May 30-At the Edge of the World

It has become typical on this expedition to pass between periods of very deep sleep, to intervals of sleeplessness. It is during those wakeful times that I was most aware of the cold. Even in the relative warmth of the tent, it was frigid. I slept wearing a wool cap, with long johns, fleece pants and jacket, wool socks, and felt booties. My sleeping bag has a hood that covers my head. Any part of my body that is snuggled in the confines of my bag is warm. My face, when it pops out of the hood, is freezing. I spend my waking time thinking of sleep, and my sleeping time dreaming vivid dreams.

The first thoughts of the day (after *Where the hell am I?*) always concerned the weather. Unfortunately, it looked bad outside this morning. It was overcast and snowing. Considering the weather, it is doubtful that we would be moving higher up today. In any event, this was a planned rest day, so we would not be going anywhere.

These rest days are scheduled to assist in our acclimatization, and without spending some time resting at high altitudes, a trip such as this is virtually impossible. Altitude has a profound effect on the human body, which performs best at sea level, which is where I live. Although many people believe that the amount of oxygen decreases as one goes up, the concentration of oxygen is constant at all altitudes up to a certain limit. However, atmospheric pressure decreases exponentially with altitude; since the gravitational pull between the earth and air molecules is greater closer to the earth, it drags the molecules closer together and increases the pressure between them, and the air molecules closer to earth also have to support the weight of those located higher above them, causing compression. Simply put, the atmosphere at higher altitudes is less dense. The atmospheric pressure at 16,000 feet is about half that at sea level, while the pressure at 29,029 feet, the height of the summit of Mt. Everest, the highest point on earth, it is about one-third the pressure at sea level. If one continued to go higher, he or she would reach a point where the altitude produces an atmospheric pressure so low that water boils at the normal temperature of the human body. This is known as the Armstrong limit, and it lies about 62,000 to 63,500 feet up. At the Armstrong limit, exposed bodily fluids, like saliva, tears and the liquids in the lungs, begin to boil and humans cannot survive without a pressurized suit. Luckily, we would not go that high.

At sea level, the atmospheric pressure causes oxygen to easily pass through the membranes of the lungs into the blood. The lower atmospheric pressure encountered in high altitude mountaineering inhibits the body's ability to process oxygen into the vascular system. The result is hypoxia, or oxygen deprivation. Hypoxia makes bad things happen. Altitude sickness, which usually occurs above 8,000 feet, produces minor symptoms including a lack of appetite, fatigue, vomiting, headache, dizziness, distorted vision, difficulty with memorizing and thinking, and irritability.

More serious cases of altitude sickness result in pneumonia-like symptoms, including edema, the accumulation of excess fluid in the body. High Altitude Cerebral Edema, or HACE, is a result of excess fluid swelling the brain. High Altitude Pulmonary Edema, or HAPE, is caused by excess fluid in the lungs. These aliments cause an increased risk of heart failure because of the stress placed on the lungs, heart, and arteries. Both cerebral edema and pulmonary edema are extremely serious and are often fatal.

Another high altitude ailment is called Cheyne-Stokes, or periodic breathing, a condition which occurs when a climber's respiration slows down as one is sleeping. I worried about this during the expedition, because I would sometime suddenly awaken at night, gasping for breath. Instead of battling for more oxygen while sleeping, the body does the opposite and respiration slows. A climber can suffer periods of apnea, when breathing stops, that can last for up to thirty seconds. The climber awakens, panting for air, with a feeling that he or she is suffocating.

Mountaineers will typically use supplemental oxygen on the upper part of high mountains like Everest and K2. The benefits of improved breathing and enhanced performance offset the disadvantage of carrying the increased load of oxygen tanks and apparatus. The question of whether climbers need oxygen to summit Mt. Everest has been hotly debated among mountaineers and medical physiologists. However, Reinhold Messner and Peter Habeler put an end to that debate in 1978 when they summited Everest without the use of supplemental oxygen. Since then, many have climbed these high mountains without the benefit of supplemental oxygen. Climbers on Denali, like us, do not use supplemental oxygen because the altitude is not as severe, and the time spent at higher altitudes is not as great.

I have experienced some of the minor symptoms of altitude sickness on each expedition I have been on, but have never been debilitated by them. For example, once on my climb in Mexico, as we sat at camp about 11,000 feet up, I suddenly developed an upset stomach and vomited without warning. I felt better immediately afterward.

The best way to guard against these maladies is to acclimatize. Acclimatization is a process in which the body adjusts to the changes taking place as higher altitudes are encountered. More red blood cells and capillaries are produced to carry more oxygen, and the lungs expand in size. Acclimatization is accomplished by a slow ascent of the mountain, and spending time at rest at increasingly higher altitudes helps the process. We followed the old climbing adage: "Climb high, sleep low." However, if any of the serious symptoms of altitude sickness arise, a rapid descent is the best medicine.

So we would spend the day resting here at the Basin Camp to acclimatize. With little to do this morning, I spent some time sightseeing. I was still amazed by the Basin Camp. Climbers were assembled in their respective campsites, in groups of three to four tents. Most of them were engaged in activities, preparing food or checking gear, as each climber stole glances at the sky. Their thoughts were focused on the weather; will it clear in sufficient time to allow a summit attempt? I remembered how many times I have heard of climbers getting stuck here, their dreams of conquering Denali dashed by bad weather. I knew that we had difficulty moving through snowstorms and wind below, and shuttered to think what that would be like up on the steeper sections of our climb.

After a leisurely breakfast, we cleaned our dishes and pots and pans. Phil poured a bit of hot water into each of them, and we used our plastic spoons to remove the larger chunks of debris, finishing the job by using gloved fingers to wipe them clean. Whatever mess was left on our gloves would soon freeze and chip off. Actually, we were living in a relatively clean and vermin-free environment; this place was even too desolate for germs to survive.

I felt the effects of the increased altitude. I was rather disoriented and felt stupid. I understood that this was normal, and did my best to concentrate, particularly when performing tasks.

We learned that the two climbers we had witnessed yesterday in Rescue Gully had made it down safely. We were happy to hear that news.

Later, we decided to walk over to the Edge of the World, which was not too far from our campsite. There, we scrambled up to the top of a large granite boulder which jutted out at the edge, and gazed out at the amazing landscape before us. The flat area of the 14,000-foot camp drops off steeply here, and it is at least a 3,000 foot drop to the glacier far below. I started feeling nervous and the exposure was very intimidating. Although I have no distinct fear of heights while standing on terra-firma, I often feel uneasy in a tall building or structure, particularly at the exposed edge. Although not on a structure, I felt anxious and uncomfortable here, so I eased my way back from the rim a bit. However, the view was overwhelming. Everything is white, with jagged peaks of various heights rising into the sky. It is both scary and beautiful. The Edge of the World definitely lived up to its billing.

While we were housekeeping back at camp, Chris returned. It was a pleasant surprise to spot his smiling face approach our camp, as he was not expected back for another day or so. Apparently, he had made extremely good time in his trip down to the Base Camp and back. He reported that Dennis had made it down and, although Dennis had great pain in his ankles as he descended, he made it without incident. Chris seemed very glad to have rejoined us, but he also appeared awfully tired. I admired his physical stamina, and realized that if it had been up to me to make that trip down and back, I wouldn't have been able to do it.

Phil decided that we should go down to the spot where we had last cached some food and gear, and bring it up here. I did not feel like moving. To some extent, I was experiencing the debilitating effects of the altitude; my head ached and I was somewhat dizzy. On top of that, I was just plain tired, and did not feel like hauling equipment back up the long hill leading into the Basin Camp. But I was quite sure that the rest of the group would not look kindly on me sitting this one out. So we assembled, roped up, and worked our way downhill to the spot at 13,500 feet where our cache was. Everyone else in the group seemed in good spirits and the conversation was lively.

When we arrived at the cache, we dug through the snow to locate our gear. It was hard to believe so much snow had accumulated in such a short time. We loaded the supplies into our packs and sleds, and then roped up for the trip back to camp. For me, it was a long and difficult uphill haul, and I wondered whether I would have the strength to go on. But I kept plugging along, one step at a time.

Back at the 14,000 foot camp, we unpacked and met in the cook tent for some hot drinks and soup. It never tasted better. The sky was clearing up, and we were anticipating moving up the mountain tomorrow.

While in the cook tent, we celebrated Chris's 21st birthday. Meegan had bought a small cake when we stopped at the grocery store, and she had carried it all the way up here in her pack. It was a real surprise for Chris as we all gathered around and sang "Happy Birthday." Several climbers from the surrounding tents came over to offer their congratulations and to share in the celebration. It was a good time.

We decided to turn in early that evening, knowing that we had a long and exhausting climb ahead of us tomorrow. Before hitting the sack, I took the snow shovel and secured the wall surrounding our tents. Inside the tent, I struggled to pull off my frozen boots. They did an incredibly good job of keeping my feet warm and dry, but they are difficult to take off or put on. I left my boots inside the tent vestibule, and retreated into the tent. My thick wool socks and polyester liner socks were damp with perspiration. I changed them, and also removed my wind and water resistant jacket and pants. Underneath those I wore a fleece jacket and pants and my long johns, and I left those on to sleep in. Although my long johns were also damp with perspiration, the heat from my body inside the sleeping bag would dry them out. At this point in the expedition, I had had on the same clothes for ten days. The odor was unpleasant, to say the least. I decided that it was too much trouble to try to change long johns, and the only item of clothing that I changed each day was my socks.

Before going to sleep, I looked out of the tent vestibule. It was an unbelievable sight. The sun was still dimly shining low in the sky, and the rock wall of the West Buttress rose sharply to my right. It cast a shadow across the tents in the camp area, while straight ahead I saw the stark face of Mt. Foraker bathed in sunshine. The scene was breathtaking, and once again made me realize that one reason we climb mountains like this is to behold the beauty of these amazing surroundings. It was a stunning but surreal image.

> *Nothing is more damning in the mountains than hubris, yet hubris is fundamental to climbing mountains. All serious mountaineers possess big egos. You cannot take on the risks and constant suffering of big mountains without one. We may talk like Buddhists, but don't be fooled, we're actually narcissists-driven, single-minded, masochistic narcissists.*
>
> Mark Jenkins – *Point of No Return*

May 31-Climbing the Dreaded Wall

The bustle of human activity woke me. I glanced around in an attempt to orient myself, wondering again: *Where am I?* Soon, I realized that people were moving about, and I heard Phil calling to awaken us. It was cold and cloudy when I dressed and left the warmth of the tent. As we assembled for breakfast, Phil told us that we would carry supplies up to the High Camp.

As we packed up our gear, I noticed many of the other groups doing the same. A welcome break in the weather would allow climbers to ascend to the upper camps from which to launch summit attempts. Although I was pleased to be breaking from the lassitude of sitting in a tent, I was also nervous about climbing the Headwall.

After packing our gear for the trip, Phil painstakingly explained the process for climbing the Headwall. He told us to step carefully and keep focused. When we got up to the fixed ropes, each of us would unhook from the rope connecting us, clip into the fixed rope with the large carabiner hooked to the front of our harnesses, and place a mechanical ascender on the fixed rope. This device slides up the rope, and then grips it tightly so that it doesn't slide back down. The ascenders will assist us in climbing the wall. At the end of the fixed rope, we will reverse the process and connect back to our regular climbing rope. This procedure had to be done carefully, as an error might prove fatal.

At this point, we abandoned our sleds. The climbing above this camp is too steep, and the sleds would simply be an aggravation. I looked up and saw a line of climbers ahead of us, some higher up and well along the Headwall. They looked like ants slowly inching upward in a winding line.

The first part of the climb was not too difficult, and we moved steadily upward and closer to the Headwall. As we did, I became increasingly more uneasy.

At the Headwall, my anxiety heightened and my heart began pounding wildly. Placing one foot cautiously in front of the other, we inched up the wall. Mike was directly ahead of me, and I wondered why he kept stopping. When I looked up past him, I saw that there was a traffic jam above him, as climbers waited in line for those above them to move. I forced myself to stay focused on the task, carefully stomping each cramponed foot into the wall as we proceeded to work our way upward.

My breathing was labored, and concentration was difficult at this height. The incline steepened as we ascended. Sections of the Headwall were indeed icy, making footing all the more difficult. I paid particular attention to unclipping myself from one fixed rope and clipping into the next one. Despite my unease, I felt as if I was doing well, and our steady progress upward was encouraging.

So as to avoid making myself more apprehensive, I made a point of not peeking down. Looking upward, I saw that we were nearing the top of the Headwall. Soon, Phil disappeared over the upper lip, and was peering down, reassuring and encouraging us to the top. Ungracefully, I clambered up and over the edge. As I stood at the top of the ridgeline, I gazed down in amazement, marveling at our accomplishment. The others joined me. With smiles on our faces, we moved away from the Headwall and down the ridgeline and took a much needed break.

The view from the top of the wall was astounding. Appearing as small dots, colorful tents stood out far below, starkly contrasting against the pure white snow. Just below me, I saw a line of climbers struggling up the Headwall, and I heard those nearest me gasping for air, just as I had done moments before.

We continued to ascend the ridgeline toward our next intended camp at 17,000 feet. It was a gradual incline and we had to scramble over steep rocks in some sections. It was here that I felt dizzy and disoriented. In a confused state, I misidentified one of the members of our team. I forced myself to take deep and regular breaths, and gradually my head cleared, but the experience was unsettling.

After plodding up to our intended campsite, an area called the High Camp, we established a cache for our gear. We enjoyed a long break before preparing to return to our camp at 14,200 feet.

Immediately after leaving the site of our cache, the route proceeds down a gradual flat slope. It ends at a ridge where the mountain drops precipitously to the glacier far below. We approached the ridgeline carefully, veered to the left, and continued downward. Soon we arrived at the top of the Headwall.

Phil spent some time explaining the proper method to descend the Headwall. Basically, all we had to do was to face forward and walk down, trusting our crampons to secure us to the mountain face. "It is a piece of cake," Phil assured us. Despite his confidence, I knew that the steep exposure would be nerve-wracking for me.

Again, I focused on my footing and carefully stomped each boot in to gain a secure hold. One step after another, we proceeded to descend. Our progress down the Headwall was much quicker than the ascent had been, but it was terrifying. Facing downhill on a steep slope and walking down is an unnatural and unnerving act, and a voice inside my head screamed for me to get down on my hands and knees and crawl. Moving slowly and judiciously, we inched down the wall. Eventually, the trail grew less inclined, and we arrived at our site in the Basin Camp without incident.

We were all in good spirits, and quite proud that we had performed well today. Confident that we had conquered the dreaded Headwall, I looked forward to moving upward toward the summit.

I am losing precious days. I am degenerating into a machine for making money. I am learning nothing in this trivial world of men. I must break away and get out into the mountains to learn the news.

John Muir

June 1-A Day of Rest

After a difficult day yesterday, I was exhausted. But sleeping at this altitude was challenging. Once again, my slumber varied from short periods of complete dead sleep to times of restless tumbling and turning. Trying to find a comfortable sleeping position was fruitless.

I peered out of the tent, and saw that the sky was overcast, and it was windy. The weather did not look good for moving upward. When Phil announced that we would likely sit tight for the day, I wasn't too disappointed.

We spent some extra time in the cook tent after breakfast, all of us dreading the retreat back into our tents. I always had mixed feelings about the days that we did not climb, and today was no exception. Although the extra rest and chance to acclimatize to the higher altitude was welcome, the boredom and drudgery of sitting in a tent all day was not. We could get up and leave the tents to eat, go to the bathroom, or shovel snow off the tents, but that required the effort of putting on boots, coats, and outer layers of clothing. I also had mixed emotions about being alone in my tent. Even though I enjoyed periods of solitude and the privacy, I sometimes missed the company of others and the extra heat in the tent produced by another person's body. In any event, I could talk to the others through the nearby tents, so it really wasn't that lonely.

I did not have much to occupy my time in the tent. I had no radio, having left it down below, but I did have a book. Prior to leaving, I bought a fiction novel about the Manhattan Project. I purposely brought a book that I believed would be entertaining without being too serious, and this book fit the bill. It was a murder mystery that took place at Los Alamos during the construction of the first atomic bomb. Although it was fictional, it was interesting and I learned about Robert Oppenheimer and other scientists and the events that occurred during that time period. I had purposely read it slowly, since I wanted it to last during these down times, but by now, I had almost finished reading the book. Often climbers will share books. One person will read several pages of a book, rip those pages out, and give them to another person to read. However, we couldn't do much of that as our group was suffering a book shortage.

By bringing myself over the edge and back, I discovered a passion to live my days fully, a conviction that will sustain me like sweet water on the periodically barren plain of our short lives.

Jonathan Waterman

June 2-Boredom Sets In

The night had been particularly cold. The morning was little better. Amid the rustling of those waking in tents, Phil stood outside and assessed the weather. It did not look good for climbing. The wind was blowing, the sky was dark gray, and it was lightly snowing. "Looks like we might have to stay put," Phil announced. His report was met with a chorus of groans. I knew that the others felt like I did. We had had enough of sitting in tents, and were ready to move on.

Today was a repeat of yesterday, but worse. Lying in my tent, tired of reading, I again studied the details of the tent walls. I scrutinized the tiny squares of the tent fabric. If I was artistic, I could have painted a picture of the interior of the tent from memory. Thinking grew weary, and always concerned the same subjects: my family and friends, how much I missed home and my office, the weather, and climbing this mountain. While at the beginning of the expedition each day was greeted with enthusiasm and awe, I now felt lethargic, drummed into submission by this accursed mountain. I wanted to either go up or down, but I didn't want to stay put.

I shot a photograph of myself, long before "selfies" were the vogue, lying in my sleeping bag. Looking back at it, I recalled how foul my mood was. My unshaven face was puffy from the effects of the altitude; peripheral edema, which causes swelling in the extremities, was the likely culprit. My lips were crusty, cracked and swollen from the cold, dry wind and brutal sun. There was a red blister on the underside of my nose. In sum, I looked terrible.

In an attempt to feel better, I told myself that this was a vacation, fantasizing that I was in an exotic location, and thinking that most hardworking people would gladly enjoy a day spent eating and lying in bed. When I told my teammates this, they groaned their disapproval. Clearly, they were no better off than I was.

I worried about the time. This was our thirteenth day on the mountain. Most Denali expeditions take between two to three weeks. We were in good shape except for the weather, but I kept thinking about the other teams that had passed us as they descended, some of them having attempted and failed to wait out the bad weather at the Basin Camp. I did not relish the thought of getting "weathered off" the mountain. All I could do was to lie back and hope for better conditions so that we could move on. I closed my eyes and silently cursed Denali's vicious weather.

People ask me, 'What is the use of climbing Mount Everest?' and my answer must at once be, 'It is of no use.' There is not the slightest prospect of any gain whatsoever. Oh, we may learn a little about the behavior of the human body at high altitudes, and possibly medical men may turn our observation to some account for the purposes of aviation. But otherwise nothing will come of it. We shall not bring back a single bit of gold or silver, not a gem, nor any coal or iron...If you cannot understand that there is something in man which responds to the challenge of this mountain and goes out to meet it, that the struggle is the struggle of life itself upward and forever upward, then you won't see why we go. What we get from this adventure is just sheer joy. And joy is, after all, the end of life. We do not live to eat and make money. We eat and make money to be able to live. That is what life means and what life is for.

George Mallory – *Climbing Everest*

June 3-To the High Camp

Phil wasted no time in making the decision: we would ascend to the High Camp today. The sky had cleared, and the prediction called for a few more days of better weather.

The mood in the camp that morning was vastly improved. We quickly ate, packed our gear, then put into a cache all of the items we would not need on the upper part of the mountain. Phil explained that we were to take only essential gear on our summit attempt, and to leave all luxuries behind. I said goodbye to my book and placed it into the duffel bag with the other items to be left there. We roped up, and once again set off for the Headwall.

Although I was very nervous during my first ascent of the Headwall, I felt better about it now, and I moved up with greater confidence than I had on my initial ascent. Slowly and steadily, up the wall we climbed, using the same method we had a few days earlier. Our climb was difficult, but uneventful.

After reaching the top of the Headwall, we took a break. A short distance ahead of us we saw Ed Hommer and his partner seated on some rocks. We cheerfully greeted them as though they were old friends. When we asked where the reporter was, they explained that they had a falling out and had parted company. Ed was not feeling particularly well; he was having some pain in his legs where the prosthetic devices attached. Despite the pain, he and his partner were forging onward. Since the reporter had gone, I assumed that we wouldn't see Ed's expedition televised.

We carefully worked our way up the steep and narrow ridge that ran along the top of the West Buttress. It was intimidating as the path was narrow with significant exposure on each side. Part of the route required scrambling over icy rocks. I was glad when we successfully navigated this section.

We reached the High Camp at 17,000 feet, and proceeded to where we had placed our cache a few days earlier. We set up our tents, built snow walls around the perimeter, put up the cook tent, and erected a restroom. We also placed some food and supplies into the cache for later use. There were a few other groups at the High Camp, all of them patiently waiting for a stab at the summit.

After setting up camp, we walked over to the edge of the flat plateau located behind our tents. The view from there was amazing. Thousands of feet below the precipitous drop off we saw the Basin Camp where we had climbed from earlier in the day. The drastic difference in altitude was remarkable, and I continued to marvel at the vast immensity of Denali. Moments like this, I thought, make climbing meaningful. We snapped some photos, each of us taking a turn posing before this incredible and majestic backdrop.

At dinner, Phil described our plans for the next day, making certain that we were paying careful attention. We would make an attempt to reach the summit. The weather was good, cold with some wind, and the forecast looked promising for tomorrow. If the weather allowed it, we would go for the top.

Phil explained that it would be our longest and most grueling day on the mountain. He described the route, the beginning part of which was visible above, and he pointed that out to us.

We would begin by a traverse of Denali Pass, a fairly steep wall rising from our camp at 17,200 feet to the ridge of Denali Pass at 18,200 feet. Denali Pass is in the shade until the afternoon, and it is extremely cold and windy. It has a notorious past; many of the falls from Denali Pass have resulted in climbers' deaths and serious injuries, and there are more accidents here than anywhere else on Denali.

The route follows the ridge from the top of Denali Pass and drops down onto a flat plateau known as the Football Field. After crossing the Football Field, the route reaches the summit ridge. The summit ridge defines classic alpine mountaineering; it is narrow with drastic, steep drop-offs on either side. The ridge rises dramatically several hundred feet to the summit at 20,310 feet.

Physically, other than a slight headache, I felt good and was encouraged that we were finally at the High Camp. I did, however, sleep very little that night, instead tossing and turning in my sleeping bag, anxiously anticipating an epic day of climbing.

*You cannot stay on the summit forever;
you have to come down again. So why
bother in the first place? Just this: What
is above knows what is below, but what
is below does not know what is above.
One climbs, one sees. One descends, one
sees no longer, but one has seen. There is
an art of conducting oneself in the lower
regions by the memory of what one saw
higher up. When one can no longer see,
one can at least still know.*

René Daumal – *Mount Analogue*

June 4-The Summit!

The final ridge leading to the summit of Denali is a quarter of a mile long. It narrows in spots to about two feet in width. To the left, there is a 600 foot drop to the plateau below; to the right lies a harrowing two mile plunge to the Ruth Glacier. As I awaken, I visualize crossing that ridge, and hope that we will walk up it to the summit before the day is done.

I must have dozed off just before our wake up call. Phil urged us out of our warm bedrolls into the icy day. The weather was cloudy and a bit windy. But we were going for the summit.

My level of excitement increased as the cobwebs of sleep slowly released my mind. Finally, after all of the preparation and planning, the patience, the hard work and effort to reach this spot, we were making our attempt to reach the top of North America.

After a quick breakfast, we roped up for the climb, this time with Phil in the lead, Meegan next, then Mike ahead of me. Chris took up the back of the rope team behind me. Following us, Romulo and Ellen were roped together as a separate team.

We began the slow traverse up Denali Pass. Although we had enough light to see, it was rather gloomy as the route was shaded from the dim sunlight of the early hour. We gradually crisscrossed the face of Denali Pass, which grew steeper as we gained altitude. My heart pounded, and although it was very cold, the physical exertion kept me warm. During a rest break, I looked down and saw our footprints winding through the snow, and I traced them back down toward our camp until I lost sight of them. We continued upward. It was strenuous work, one slow, deliberate step at a time, but we gradually rose to the top of Denali Pass.

At the ridgeline on the top of the Pass, we moved up through some rock outcroppings. We eventually reached the Football Field, and were relieved by the relative flatness of this section of the climb.

I felt very good. I stayed focused and forced myself to breathe hard to maximize my oxygen intake. Mike, climbing just above me, started struggling. I think the altitude was getting to him.

As we began the climb up to the summit ridge after crossing the Football Field, Mike stopped frequently. He told Phil he couldn't go on. I heard Phil urge him, not so gently, telling Mike that he knew he had it in his legs, he just needed to get it right in his head. Mike breathed hard, and, with a determined effort, continued the slow surge upward.

As we neared the summit ridge, we took off our packs and secured them in the snow. We would not need them up on the summit.

The summit ridge on Denali is extraordinary. The route runs along this ridge line to the summit, and we followed the path in the snow as it gradually wound up toward the top. As we creeped along the summit ridge, I gazed down to the right at the steep face of Mt. Huntington, which rises to a height of 12,240 feet. The drop from either side of the ridge is formidable, and it was intimidating to be there. I carefully concentrated on my footing, trying not to lose focus by sightseeing. I had nothing on my mind except this: *one cautious step, then another.* I allowed no other thoughts to distract me. We progressed onward and upward, one step after another, with encouraging words from Phil and Chris. Mike was his old self, climbing with renewed vigor. All of us were energized as we realized that we were within grasp of our goal.

There were no other climbers behind us. A few had passed us going in the opposite direction on their way down from the summit. They seemed extremely tired but very happy, each of them urging us upward, telling us "Good work," or "You're almost there," words that were very motivating and encouraging to hear.

I was gasping for air, partly the effect of the altitude, but also in the excited anticipation of reaching the summit. My mind began to wander and I thought of all the work I had put into this, the days spent patiently waiting in tents, all of my concerns about whether I would be strong enough, physically and mentally, to make the climb. It was overwhelming, and, as I began to move up the steeper part of the ridge at the doorstep of the summit, I began to softly weep and cold tears ran down my frozen cheeks. I don't know why it affected me so strongly, but as I stepped up to join Phil, Mike and Meegan on the summit, I was overcome with emotion. I couldn't believe it. I had reached the summit--the highest point in North America.

Chris joined us at the top, and we all hugged, cheered, and took photographs. My youngest daughter had given me a small banner from her high school, and I attempted to hold it up for a summit photo, but it was very windy so I grasped it tightly against me so that it would not blow away. I then realized how blustery and cold it was.

The summit itself is a bit unremarkable. It is a relatively flat, snow-covered area about the size of a small vehicle. Looking around, I could see that there was nothing higher, and nowhere to go from here but down. The view from the top was amazing and awe-inspiring. Although it was overcast, I could still see the range of mountains below me. Innumerable peaks and crags, all white with snow except for the gray granite areas too steep for the snow to hold, trailed off in the far distance until disappearing beyond my range of vision. Clouds streamed through the sky below us, while those above cast a grey pall over us. I looked down at the summit ridge we had just ascended, seeing our footprints along its razor-sharp edge, and followed its impressive path downward. I couldn't stop smiling; I was elated.

I recalled my childhood dreams, my mountaineering fantasies now realized. I thought of my family and how they had encouraged me to do my best, confident that I would reach the summit. Now, here I stood, overwhelmed by the realization that I had accomplished my goal. For a brief, remarkable moment, as I stood there alone, I relished the feeling of being the highest living creature standing atop the North American continent.

Phil broke my reverie. It was about 4:00 PM. He stated that it was getting late, and even though we had been on the summit for only about half an hour, we needed to move down before the weather got bad. We packed up our cameras, ate snacks and drank some water, then began the descent.

We followed the same route back down the mountain. On the way up, the guides had marked our path with wands so that we could find our way back if the weather deteriorated. It was overcast and cold, but otherwise the weather was passable. Proceeding down the summit ridge, attempting to step cautiously despite the huge grin on my face, we encountered some ascending climbers. We happily told them, "Almost there," and "Not too far to go."

Getting to the summit is only the half-way point of an expedition; we still have to safely return to the start. In quoting the well-known mountaineer Ed Viesturs,

Phil said: "It's a round trip. Getting to the summit is optional; getting down is mandatory." The descent is more dangerous than an ascent; more accidents happen during the climb back down. Climbers are tired and usually less focused after returning from the summit, they are going faster because they are going downhill, while the risks are all the same as they are on the climb up. Again, I tried to stay focused on my footing.

After reaching the top of Denali Pass, the camp at 17,200 feet soon became visible in the far distance below. It was a welcome sight. Plunging our cramponed feet into the snow, we plodded downward at a quick pace, and arrived safely back at camp.

We were joyous as we had hot drinks and a warm meal. As we continued to congratulate each other, Phil told us that we had accomplished a great achievement, and that we should all be proud of how well we performed. I knew that we had to safely return to the Base Camp, but for now, I had no worries and all was well.

We had been climbing for well over twelve hours, and I was completely exhausted. As did the others, I happily scrambled into my tent, looking forward to a well-deserved rest. As I sat there reflecting on the experience, I thought of these poetic words to capture my feelings:

> *Risen with toil,*
> *above the soil,*
> *where lies the maddening roar.*

Rapt by the thrill,
Atop this great hill,
Above the eagle's soar.

One more time I thought, *I made it to the top of Denali.* Then, with the huge grin still creasing my face, I fell into an exhausted sleep.

Chris, Dennis, Mike, Meegan and author at hotel in Talkeetna

Getting ready for the flight from Talkeetna to Base Camp

Approaching Denali Base Camp. Runway is to the right

First Camp. Route rises up in center

Tents at camp one

Approaching the Basin Camp. Cache at left

Author "on the throne" at Basin Camp

View from "The Edge of the World" at Basin Camp

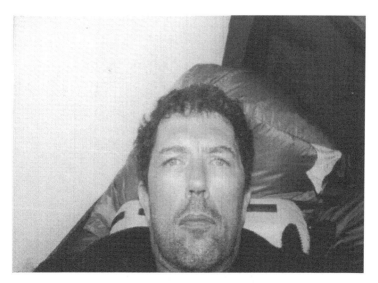

The author in tent at Basin Camp

View of ridge leading up to High Camp

View of Basin Camp from edge of High Camp

Climbers approaching the summit ridge

On the Summit: Phil, Mike, Meegan, Chris and author

If the conquest of a great peak brings moments of exultation and bliss, which in the monotonous, materialistic existence of modern times nothing else can approach, it also presents great dangers. It is not the goal of grand alpinism to face peril, but it is one of the tests one must undergo to deserve the joy of rising for an instant above the state of crawling grubs. But soon we have to start the descent. Suddenly I feel sad and despondent. I am well aware that a mountaineering victory is only a scratch in space. But in spite of this, how sad I feel at leaving that crest! On this proud and beautiful mountain we have lived hours of fraternal, warm and exciting nobility. Here for a few days we have ceased to be slaves and have really been men. It is hard to return to servitude.

Lionel Terray – *Conquistadors of the Useless*

June 5-Resting at High Camp

It did not sound good. I awoke to the rattle of my tent walls, as they were being pummeled by ferocious winds. Realizing that it was morning, I waited to hear Phil's instructions for the day. After a while, Phil went out and gauged the weather conditions. Based on the weather report, and what he observed, Phil told us we would have to hunker down and ride out a storm.

This time, I did not mind sitting in my tent for a day. I was still worn out from our efforts yesterday, by far our most strenuous day on the mountain. I ventured out of my tent only if necessary, which was to go to the bathroom, eat with the others in the cook tent, or to knock snow off my tent and to fortify the snow blocks around it. I felt very lazy and lethargic, and forced myself to get out of the relative warmth of my shelter. Exercise is necessary at this height to avoid altitude sickness, and I did my best to move about, notwithstanding the difficulty of the cramped quarters.

One of the better decisions I had made was to bring an ample supply of toilet tissue with me. Toilet paper is a hot commodity on Denali, and at this stage of the expedition, others' supplies are running low. I loaned some to the others in my group as they needed it, but always checked to make sure I kept enough for myself.

The wind continued throughout the day, and, as usual, it was very cold. I dozed off and on all day and into the night. By the end of the day, I had enough of sitting in the tent and hoped that we would be able to descend in the morning. I was looking forward to going home.

The rope connecting two men on a mountain is more than nylon protection; it is an organic thing that transmits subtle messages of intent and disposition from man to man; it is an extension of the tactile senses, a psychological bond, a wire along which currents of communication flow.

Trevanian – *The Eiger Sanction*

June 6-Tragedy Strikes

The weather had improved by morning. When I crawled out of my tent, I saw other climbing teams preparing to move on. Again, Phil listened to the weather report over the radio. It appeared that we would begin the climb down today.

Indeed, we packed up for the descent. Still ecstatic from having reached the top of Denali, we laughed and joked as we prepared to go home. We loaded our backpacks with everything we had at the High Camp. Phil was first on the rope, with me behind him, Mike behind me, followed by Meegan and Chris at the back end. As we stood in line ready to proceed, the weather was cooperating. It was overcast, but the wind had died down, just occasionally gusting. Some other groups started out ahead of us, and I saw others packing up for their descents.

The route down was the same that we had ascended. Looking back to make sure we were ready, Phil nodded and then led the way, and we began walking in a straight line along a gradual decline toward the ridge at 17,000 feet. It was snowing lightly, and the wind blew in sporadic gusts. We rounded a corner where the slope steepened, and stepped up toward the ridge. The wind became much stronger. It was not constant, but when it blew, I felt its force.

Phil stopped and looked back, yelling for us to be careful. Again, we inched forward. From here, we would leave the relatively gradual downward slope we had descended from the High Camp, hike left onto the ridge, and then scramble along the ridgeline down to the top of the Headwall. I looked out and, although it was overcast, I was able to see that the slope below us dropped steeply. From here, it is nearly a three mile drop to the tundra below.

The wind continued to blow intermittently. Stepping forward, my body rocked as the wind suddenly gusted. As I took another step forward, the wind shook me and my crampon slipped on the icy surface. Suddenly, I pitched forward and crashed down on my shoulder. In a blur, I slid downward, head first and face down, my body skating along the rock-hard ice and snow. Realizing that I was in trouble, I reacted.

Beginning with my first climb on Mt. Rainier several years earlier, we had trained in the art of self-arresting, a skill we practiced each time we climbed. The goal of a self-arrest is to slow down or stop your body from skating downwards by jamming the point of the ice axe into the surface of the ice or snow, and tightly holding on. There is a defined technique for each position that your body is in. Sliding headfirst is one of the worst ways to go.

Acting almost instinctively, I hammered the sharp end of my ice axe into the frozen surface of the mountain. It held tight, and my legs swung down so that I was now facing uphill. I slammed the front points of the crampons on each of my feet into the frozen wall. I looked around in an attempt to orient myself. I realized that I was pinned to the flank of Denali, held in place by my ice axe and crampons, and still roped together with my climbing partners. The wind was now blowing strongly, gusting powerfully at times, and it began snowing. It seemed as if I was in a snowy hurricane. Visibility became horrible, as it was virtually impossible to see much of anything.

Phil was located up above me to my right, but I could not see him. Following the other end of the rope connected to my harness, I saw it rise up above me to my left and over the lip of the ridgeline from where I had fallen. I knew that Mike was on the rope behind me, and that Phil was holding fast on the rope in front of me, so I told myself that I was secure from falling further. Although I knew my partners were there, I could not see anyone.

I also could not hear much of anything. When the wind gusted, I heard nothing but its roar. When the wind died down, I heard Phil's voice to my right. He was screaming to me, but I could not discern his words.

Every time the wind thundered across my body, it felt like I was being sucked off the mountain by an invisible vacuum. I grasped my ice axe tightly with both hands and forced the toe points of my crampons into the wall with every bit of strength I had. My legs began to tremble as a result of the effort. Time seemed to stand still; I felt as if I was trapped on this steep mountain slope.

Growing fatigued, and with my mind numbed and muddled by the altitude and the circumstances, I was ready to give up. I became increasingly confused, frustrated and lethargic. I simply did not know what to do.

But I thought of my family. I could not let them down. *Somehow*, I told myself, *I would have to find a way out of this dire dilemma, and I would do it for them.* I attempted to focus my mind on extracting myself from this mess.

While in this stupor, the wind blasted again. I looked up the instant I heard the shriek of a woman's voice from above, and had the sense that something had blown past me on my left side. It was just a blur in my peripheral vision in extremely poor visibility, but I felt as something had dashed by me. I tried to imagine what had happened.

The sound of Phil's voice broke my trance. "Stand up," he shouted. Muffled by the winds, I heard him command again: "Stand up!" Focusing all of my attention, I released one foot from the slope, placed it flat down into the ice, and then did the same with the other foot. The crampons on my boot bottoms held fast.

I yanked my ice axe from the side of the mountain, and, grasping it tightly so as to not lose it, sunk the point into the ice and used it to maintain my balance. I forced myself into an awkward upright position. Hunched over, I shakily took one small step up and forward, and then another, slamming my ice axe and crampons into the frigid surface each time. The rope holding me was secure and tight, but I felt as if I could tumble down the cliff at any moment. With every bit of concentration and strength I had, I forced my body upward toward the ridge, fighting fear the entire time. After what seemed like an eternity, I reached the top of the ridge where I was met by other climbers who grabbed ahold of me.

By now, it had escalated into a raging blizzard. I heard people screaming, other voices shouting commands, and saw the dim forms of climbers rushing about in a blur. I tried to comprehend what had happened. I realized that Phil had arrived, and he quickly un-roped himself and joined a small group of other climbers. All of them appeared to be animated and excited. The scene was chaotic and surreal.

"What happened?" I asked of no one in particular. I saw Mike and Meegan, who were both tremendously upset. "It was Chris," Meegan cried, "Chris fell!" I could not believe what I heard. It made no sense to me. "What happened?" I asked again. They explained that Chris had un-roped himself from the back of the rope team, proceeded to the ridge line, and looked down to see what had happened. A sudden gust of wind had blown him down the face of the mountain.

The dreadful details emerged much later. When I fell, Phil used a rock as protection, and took all of the slack out of the rope so that I would not fall further. As Phil was shouting directions to me, Chris approached Meegan, who was tied into the rope directly in front of him, unclipped his rope from her harness, and began descending from the ridge top toward me. Meegan told Chris to stay tied in to her harness, and when he didn't, she yelled ahead for him to clip into Mike's harness, as Mike was tied in ahead of her and nearest to the ridge. Likely concerned for my safety, Chris advanced to help without securing himself to the rope. Perhaps he slipped on the icy surface and lost his footing, but in any event, he was blown off the ridge and the wind catapulted him downward.

Several groups of climbers were behind us as we had descended toward the ridge. They converged to lend assistance. Some of them had erected a tent, and a young man led me to it. He told me to get inside to warm up. As I sat there alone, I tried without success to comprehend what had taken place. It was like a bizarre nightmare, and I fully expected that I would awaken and all would be well.

Another climber leapt into the tent behind me. He asked me my name, told me his, and said that he was a firefighter from Florida who was climbing with another team. I asked about Chris, and all he knew was that several climbing guides were trying to work their way down the steep cliff where Chris had fallen in an attempt to find him. He asked me about injuries, and I then realized that my shoulder hurt where I had landed on it when I toppled over. He checked it, and said that it was bruised, but not broken or bleeding. I was able to move it without too much pain. He told me to bundle up and stay warm, and left the tent.

As I sat alone in the tent, I realized how cold I was. I was shivering, every part of my body chilled to the bone. My fingers were the worst; they were actually aching. I hunkered down in the sleeping bag, begging for warmth.

Emotionally, I was a mess. I knew that Chris's situation was dire. I also realized that it was my fault. Balled in a fetal position alone in a tent somewhere on the upper reaches of Denali, I cried uncontrollably.

Approaching voices caught my attention. Soon, Mike and Meegan appeared at the entrance to the tent. They climbed in, and explained that Phil and some guides from other expeditions had gone down the mountainside where Chris had fallen in a rescue attempt. However, the storm made their task nearly impossible. The blinding snow made for poor visibility, while the voracious winds made moving on the steep icy slope tricky and dangerous. Given the circumstances, there was little hope for Chris.

I could see that Meegan and Mike were also extremely distraught. In one sense, I wanted to be alone in my misery, but on the other hand, it was good to have others to share my grief. "It was my fault," I told them. "This would not have happened except for my mistake." They told me not to blame myself, and that Chris had un-roped himself and then walked past them to see why we had stopped. Meegan explained that she had watched as Chris approached the edge, and she screamed as she saw Chris being hurdled off the mountain by the sudden gust of wind. I realized then that what I had seen off to my side was Chris as he flew down the steep slope past me. Despite having a better understanding of what occurred, I felt miserable.

After a while, Phil arrived with Ellen and Romulo. Phil told us that he and other well-experienced mountain guides had done their best to find Chris but, due to the appalling weather conditions, they were unable to locate him. Phil said that we had done nothing wrong, and that it was important for us to work together to get safely home. I had not realized it, but the tent we were in was set up back at the High Camp at 17,200 feet where we had begun the day. Phil, Ellen and Romulo set up another tent. Phil explained that we would ride out the storm with three of us in each of the two tents. These tents are designed to hold two people comfortably, so it would be cramped with three occupants, but we did not anticipate staying at the High Camp for very long. Meegan squeezed in between Mike and I, while Ellen and Romulo joined Phil in the other tent. Phil brought us some hot water and some food, and, while none of us had any appetite, we did our best to eat and drink, and the hot fluids helped warm my frozen body.

The night passed miserably, and sleep was impossible. The jubilation I had felt after reaching Denali's summit was replaced with dark despair. We talked about Chris and the accident throughout the night. Making it the more painful for us was the realization that Chris could have gone home when he took Dennis back to Base Camp. Phil had given Chris the option of leaving, but he elected to return to be with us. We all loved Chris, but because he was closer to Mike and Meegan, his absence was having a profound effect on them. Needless to say, it was a wretchedly long and sleepless night for all of us.

He cried in a whisper at some image, at some vision--he cried out twice, a cry that was no more than a breath: "The horror! The horror!"

Joseph Conrad – *Heart of Darkness*

June 7-Sorrowful Day at the High Camp

There is no difference between night and day. The inside of the tent remained light throughout the night, darkening slightly during the dusk hours. Sleep had come in brief intervals, and each time I awakened from the stupor, it was with a sorrowful recollection of the day's events. Try as I may, I could not shake the thoughts of the vile events from my mind.

Any thought of moving to the lower camps was dispelled by the weather. Again, it was windy and snowing. Phil seemed as anxious as we were to move out of here, but when he poked his head into our tent to give us hot water to make drinks, he told us that we would have to sit tight. He did say that we would keep an eye on the weather, and if the storm passed, we would make our move. I did not think I could sit through another day. At this altitude, our bodies continued to deteriorate, the boredom was mind-numbing, and we were all in depressed states of mind. I realized that it would be foolhardy to attempt to descend in this weather, and resigned myself to try to keep a positive attitude.

Mike and Meegan were good company, and I got to know them much better through our forced stay together in the tent. I admired them for undertaking this venture together, and told them that if they could survive this adventure, then their upcoming marriage could endure anything.

I continued to struggle to understand what happened to Chris. Logically, I could assemble the facts in my mind, and I comprehended the events, but I could not fathom why he was dead. It still seemed like a strange nightmare, and it made no sense to me. I questioned my decision to embark on this journey on this deadly mountain. That made no sense to me either.

To alleviate the weakening of our bodies, and to ease the boredom, we took turns venturing out of the tent from time to time. Of course, it was a major undertaking each time we did this. We had to put on frozen boots, heavy mittens and outer clothes, unzip the tent door, jump out into the blast of wind and cold, then zip the tent door back up as quickly as possible. We went out to shovel snow off the tents, to go to the bathroom, and to stretch out. Although it was a miserable process, doing this helped not only physically, but psychologically as well. It broke the monotony of lying in the tent, and it gave me a chance to think about the tasks at hand, rather than to sit in the tent worrying about our plight.

Mike tried once again to contact his students, but his efforts proved fruitless. It had been a long time since he had communicated with his class, and Mike was concerned because he knew that his students would be worried.

As the day wore on, despite the lack of an appetite, I forced myself to drink water and eat snacks. Not intending to be here for long, we did not assemble the mess tent and ate in our tents. Phil brought us slices of salami, cheese (which I dislike but ate), apples and other goodies. We also had our individual supplies of candy bars. I knew that we were fine, but worried that if the storm continued, we would run out of food or fuel, which we needed for the stoves to cook and to melt snow for drinking water. We had stored food and fuel at the lower camps below us for the trip back down, and we had some here, but none of the groups at the High Camp were stocked with more than a few days' worth of supplies. The winds continued to rock the tents, and I wondered how much they could handle before being shredded apart. Even though we were in no immediate danger, when sitting in a tent under these circumstances, one's mind tends to dwell on the worst.

Mike, Meegan and I continued to talk about Chris and the horrific tragedy throughout the day. It was almost as if we were discussing someone's awful nightmare, and the realization that it was all too true sickened me. We realized that at this point there was no hope for his rescue, and that Chris had fallen to his demise.

When the weather did not improve, it became certain that we would have to stay here for another long day. Morbidly, in my despondent state of mind, I began to believe that we were trapped here, that in fact we could not get back down and no one could rescue us. The situation was probably not that dire, but I surrendered to the idea that my life would end here, frozen and buried in a tent at 17,200 feet up on Denali.

It is the part of men to fear and tremble,
When the most mighty gods by tokens send
Such dreadful heralds to astonish us.

William Shakespeare – *Julius Caesar*

June 8-Descending the Deadly Ridge

During the night, the wind had diminished. Looking outside, I saw that it was no longer snowing. Phil had arisen earlier and walked out across the plateau toward the ridgeline. When he returned, he told us that we would pack up and move out. Although my mood improved slightly, I still felt numbed and drained of emotions. Mechanically, I joined the others in packing up our belongings.

Chris's absence was conspicuous as we lined up as we had before. We attached the rope to our harnesses and set out on our journey down, Phil in the lead. Although it was overcast and breezy, it was not snowing and the conditions seemed favorable.

As we neared the ridgeline, my heart pounded and my breathing grew more labored. I willed myself to focus on my footing and made sure that my crampons were stomped securely into the ice and snow. When we reached the ridge and turned left to proceed down it, I magnified my cautious efforts. We inched downward, my heart pounding as I tried to force myself to watch my steps, to stay focused, and not to think about the horrible accident that had happened right here just two days before.

The renowned mountaineers, Lou and Jim Whittaker, had an incident occur near this same spot. The Whittakers had not climbed Mt. McKinley, so they went there in 1960. Along with their friends and climbing partners Pete Schoening and John Day, they reached the summit in what was then an incredible record time of four days. However, they had not properly acclimatized, and began having difficulties on the descent from the summit. All roped together, they fell from near the top of Denali Pass at 18,000 feet, and slid down the wall about 500 feet. While the Whittakers were shaken up but otherwise uninjured, John Day had fractured and dislocated both ankles, and Pete Schoening was semiconscious, having taken a blow to the head.

They were at 17,300 feet and the temperature was 35 below zero. Since John Day could not walk, they dug a hole in the snow, put him into two sleeping bags, and secured him in the hole. They began hiking toward their tent, which was at their camp located below them. In Lou Whittaker's words:

> We came to a ridge at 16,800 feet, above our third camp at 16,200 on the West Buttress. We were at a place where the ridge becomes extreme and you have to go either to the left or the right. Going to the right led to the 3,000-foot wall above Peters Glacier. The route to the left sloped down a 1,500-foot wall toward our

camp. I was about 60 feet behind Jim and Pete. There were no footprints, but my Boy Scout memory training was still intact. I had memorized the slope on the way up. I was quite sure that we were to go to the left of the ridge, and my twin felt the same. Pete said no, we go to the right.

After a brief argument, Pete went right and the Whittakers went left, in the same direction that we were then heading. They made it back to the tent and rested for a short while. Realizing that Pete Schoening was disoriented, Lou Whittaker roused himself to go get him. Jim had been beaten up in the fall and was not doing well, so he remained in the tent to rest. Lou ascended the route and, after a while, found Pete sitting on a rock outcrop just below the edge of the 3,000-foot cliff that rose above the Peters Glacier, his feet dangling over the edge. Lou carefully assisted Pete down to the camp.

John Day was rescued after a dramatic helicopter landing near the spot he was dug into. The other members of the party were able to safely descend the mountain.

I believe that my fall, and Chris Hooyman's subsequent plummet down the icy wall, happened near same place as that described by Lou Whittaker, as his narrative sounded eerily similar. Sadly, the consequences for us were much worse than they had been for the Whittakers' party.

We continued to work our way along the rugged edge of the ridge line, gradually and deliberately advancing toward the top of the Headwall. Eventually, we reached that point without incident. Phil directed us to take a short rest there, and we drank some water and nibbled on candy bars. While I faced the previous descents of the Headwall with great apprehension, I was now glad to be there. I knew that the safety and relative comfort of the Basin Camp was just below.

Our break was brief, and after reminding us to proceed carefully, Phil started down the Headwall. Again, I marched cautiously, one step at a time, making sure that my footing was secure. With immense relief, we slowly worked our way back down to the Basin Camp. After some difficulty locating our cache, which had been buried under the deep snow, we set up our tents.

Although I had not realized it at the time, as we descended, four National Park Service rangers ascended from 14,200 feet up to the site of Chris's plunge. There, they put 900 feet of fixed rope down Chris's fall line, and two rangers went down and searched for hours. They found nothing.

While relieved to have made it safely down to the Basin Camp, Phil's face revealed his pained emotions. Almost immediately, some climbers approached Phil and spoke with him in hushed tones. Phil told us that he had to leave for a few minutes, and walked away with them.

When he returned, Phil explained that he had been to the ranger station at the Basin Camp to discuss the details of the accident. He told us that they were searching for Chris, but the hunt had been hampered by bad weather. He asked us to go to the ranger station and tell the rangers what we knew about the accident. So Meegan, Mike and I trod across the broad plateau of the Basin Camp to the ranger station.

A ranger greeted us, and asked us to come in one at a time. When it was my turn, I entered and sat on a chair. There were a couple of young men who asked me to tell them all that I knew and had observed about the incident. They were polite, quietly understanding and patient, one of them jotting notes as I spoke. After explaining what happened, I left, and we silently returned to camp. It was difficult for me to talk about Chris's accident, but I realized that would not be the last time I would do so.

It was all still very strange and dreamlike. I could not yet fully comprehend what had happened. I just wanted to awaken from this dreadful bad dream and escape from the grasp of this mountain.

Sitting outside my tent in camp, I felt as if we were the focus of attention. I could see climbers in other groups looking our way and talking among themselves. Although I doubt it was the case, in my mind I believed that I was the center of the attention, that the other climbers there had identified me as the culprit, the cause of Chris's death. More than anything, I just wanted to get away. I wanted to go home.

There is no exquisite beauty without some strangeness in the proportion.

Edgar Allan Poe (quoting Francis Bacon) – *Ligeia*

June 9-Down to the Base Camp

Better weather arrived in the morning, so we decided to move down the hill. Phil again spoke with other guides and a ranger, and then told us we needed to pack up. Our plan was to hike all the way from here down to the Denali Base Camp. It would be a long day, but I was in fairly good spirits knowing that we were going to be homeward bound.

Thus, we trudged across the Basin Camp toward Windy Corner. We marched downward in quietude until we arrived at one of our caches. There, we loaded up the gear we had left behind, ate some of our food, and then moved on. It was a miserably long day, exhausting hours of plodding along, and we spoke little, each of us enmeshed in our thoughts. Even though we trekked through some of the most spectacular scenery on the planet, I was indifferent. I became annoyed. My pack was uncomfortable. I was tired. I could not wait to reach the Base Camp. Apathetically, I crept along.

Although it seemed as if we were going slow, we made good progress in descending, plunging down the mountain at a fairly rapid pace. It was amazing that we had covered so much ground, while the ascent had been insufferably slow.

One of the disappointing features of a descent of Denali is the aptly named Heartbreak Hill. Although the large part of the descent is downhill, the section leading directly into Base Camp is a gradual incline. After suffering an exhausting day descending the mountain, most climbers become utterly frustrated by Denali's last punch. It was physically and mentally trying to overcome this last obstacle. Eventually, though, with Phil urging us on as we struggled uphill, Base Camp came into view, and with renewed enthusiasm, we strode into camp.

The Base Camp was crowded. Most of the occupants were like us, waiting for their flights off the mountain. Others, however, were starting their expeditions. We set up our tents, ate some food, and relaxed. It felt good to be here.

After getting settled in, Phil went to the Base Camp manager's tent to check in. When he returned, he was met by a couple of officials from Rainier Mountaineering, Inc. I am certain that they were there to discuss the accident, as well as to check on us. Other than being emotionally and physically exhausted, we were fine.

The challenge then became getting off the mountain. Phil had radioed in to Geeting to request the planes to come the next day. Except for the tents, sleeping bags and other essentials we would need to spend the night, we began packing up our gear for the trip home. After dinner, we sat around for a bit and talked about our expedition. Then, it was off to sleep, with thoughts of a steak dinner, beer, a hot shower and a warm bed dancing through my mind.

That evening, I shared a tent with Phil. I could see that he was very distraught. He said that in all of his years of guiding, he never had a client seriously injured or killed. I thought of what a remarkable record that was. Phil told me that I had done nothing wrong, and it made me feel better to know that he did not believe that I caused Chris's fall. He sadly shook his head, and I knew that he could not stop thinking about Chris and the tragedy that ended his life.

I wondered if this incident summoned Phil's memories of the death of another climber who was close to him. In 1982, Lou Whittaker led an American expedition through China to climb Mt. Everest from the north side of the mountain. In addition to Jim Wickwire and a few other experienced mountaineers, he selected several experienced guides from Rainier Mountaineering as part of the climbing team. Phil Ershler was one of them. Another was Marty Hoey, a preeminent female climber. Hoey had worked with RMI as a guide for years, and was well known for her climbing abilities, strength and stamina. She was also extremely personable and well-liked by climbing clients and other guides. Marty was the only female in the Everest climbing team, but was as capable and able as any of the male climbers.

Working on a rope team with Jim Wickwire as part of the summit party, she and Wickwire approached a rock at about 26,000 feet up. They were just below two other climbers on a 45 degree ice slope, and visibility was poor. The climbers above called out for some rope, and Wickwire began unraveling it. Hearing a snap, Wickwire looked below him to see Hoey falling backwards down the slope. She slid head-first backwards down the icy incline, attempting unsuccessfully to grab the fixed rope as she skidded. Marty fell to her death, crashing 6,000 feet down the Great Couloir all the way to the glacier below.

Marty Hoey's death had a tremendous impact on Lou Whittaker, Jim Wickwire, Phil Ershler and the other expedition members. Lou Whittaker later wrote: "After the rage came the disappointment, sadness, and incredible loneliness. I felt like the heart of the expedition had stopped beating. Many of us questioned whether mountaineering was something that we would follow in the future."

After her fall, Wickwire saw Marty's ice axe and harness, which was lying there open and attached to the fixed rope. It appeared that she had neglected to loop her harness belt back through the buckle, which would have held her harness fast and prevented her fall. This method of securing the harness was drilled into us by our mountain guides and is something that we were always reminded to do. In reviewing photographs after the incident, they learned that Hoey sometimes failed to follow this procedure.

Although I did not speak with Phil about that incident, I knew that it had to trouble him, and I am sure that he was keenly aware of the similarities between Chris Hooyman and Marty Hoey, and their accidental deaths. Both were proficient climbing guides, and their climbing accidents appear to have been caused by human error; in Chris's case, he unroped himself, while Marty did not properly secure her harness. And both were friendly, popular and well-liked individuals, whose deaths left many grieving in pain.

When you part from your friend,
you grieve not;
for that which you love most in him
may be clearer in his absence,
as the mountain to the climber
is clearer from the plain.

Kahlil Gibran - *The Prophet*

June 10-Stuck on Denali

A gloomy grey sky hung over the distant mountain peaks as I stepped out of my tent. The wind was blustery, but not awful. Phil said that we would have to wait to see if the planes could get through to retrieve us.

I stared at the landing strip, a rutted line of snow and ice along the glacier, willing the weather to allow our airplanes to arrive. We heard the distant growl of the engine of a plane, and saw some climbers in another group hurry excitedly toward the runway. The plane bounced to a landing and, after the climbers loaded up, they took off. But that was it for the day. The weather deteriorated, and no one else was able to fly from the Base Camp.

Once again, we spent the day sitting around camp, taking an occasional sightseeing tour to relieve the boredom. And once again, I burrowed into my sleeping bag, hoping that I would be gone from Denali tomorrow. As time slowly ticked by, I grew despondent, feeling as if the mountain had me trapped. I wanted to get off, but she wouldn't let me go.

It is good to have an end to journey toward; but it is the journey that matters in the end.

Ursula K. Le Guin

June 11-Flying to Talkeetna

I woke up with renewed hope. The weather seemed to have improved by morning, although grey skies lingered. Phil again radioed the flight service, and Geeting Aviation gave us good news. They would try to send the planes in for us today. However, they wanted to wait a bit to assure that weather allowed them to fly.

Again, I was on the edge of my seat. I wanted nothing more than to go home. I was beaten physically and emotionally. So once again, I stared at the runway and hoped.

The day passed again much the same as yesterday. Phil told us to pack everything up, including the tents, so that we would be ready to go. We perked up when we heard the drone of a buzzing plane coming in, and when it landed, three climbers from another group pitched their gear in and bounded aboard. The engine rumbled away. I tried to be happy for them, and felt guilty when I didn't. *That should have been us*, I jealously thought.

A few more planes landed and took off in similar fashion. I was beginning to lose hope that ours' would arrive, as the hour was getting late. Phil called us together. Meegan, Mike, Romulo, Ellen and I stood in a semi-circle. "Geeting is sending someone to get us, but the weather is still dicey," he said. "Let's be ready to go."

As we waited, Phil spoke privately with an RMI guide. Afterward, we overheard mention of a serious accident that day on Mt. Rainier. Later, I learned how severe it was.

An RMI guided team was descending from the summit of Mt. Rainier. Two rope teams were clipped into the same fixed rope. They descended from the summit, and were at an altitude of 11,200 feet. There, the climbers were hit by an avalanche from above, causing them to tumble down to a steep, icy rock cliff. Thrown by the force of the avalanche, all of the climbers were strewn out across the cliff, and one, Patrick Nestler, fell substantially further down than the others. Sadly, Nestler died from the exposure. Through a Herculean rescue effort, all of the other climbers, nine in total, were saved, some with minor injuries, while other were more seriously hurt. Given what happened on our expedition, I am sure that the report of the Mt. Rainier incident added to Phil's misery.

Time came to a standstill as we waited for the plane. Finally, after what seemed like hours, we heard the distinctive whine of the small ski-plane's engine. Phil told us that because the weather conditions had deteriorated, only one plane could get through this evening. Thus, only three of us could go, while the others would have to remain behind at Base Camp to await planes the next day. We began a discussion of which three climbers would fly out.

Phil said that he would remain for the next flight. All of us offered to stay, though I silently prayed that I would leave then. Finally, he decided that Ellen, Meegan and I would take this plane.

The pilot guided the bouncing plane along the landing strip. We hurled our bags in as soon as the door opened, and then quickly jumped aboard. We waved goodbye to those left behind and bounded along, the plane struggling to gain speed for the takeoff. Eventually, we lifted into the gray clouds. I could see that the pilot was completely focused on controlling the aircraft, which bobbed furiously in the invisible winds. Through leaden skies, the plane groaned to gain altitude as it passed through the majestic mountain peaks, bouncing roughly as it did so. Under normal conditions, I would have been terrified on such a bumpy flight, but I was calm then, my sensations numbed by the events of the past few days. *Hell,* I thought, *if we crash and I die here, so be it. This is not a bad place to go.*

The flight continued through the darkening grey skies. Eventually, we reached cruising altitude and continued onward toward Talkeetna. Silently, we all gazed out of the small windows at the incredible scenery of these beautiful mountains, each of us lost in our own deep thoughts.

We bobbed to a safe landing on the paved airstrip in Talkeetna. We all cried out in joy, leapt from the plane, and removed our duffel bags. I wanted to kiss the ground. As I grabbed some gear and walked toward the hanger, I felt an odd sensation, and realized that this was the first time in several weeks that I was not walking on snow. The familiar hollow "crunch, crunch" sound of walking on snow, much like the sound of grinding Styrofoam, was gone, as I felt nothing but solid ground underfoot. It was a very strange feeling.

We loaded the group gear in the hanger. Doug Geeting welcomed us in the office, and told us that the other planes had not been able to get to the Base Camp. Phil, Mike and Romulo would be stuck there at least until tomorrow. We gathered our personal gear, and then made the short walk to the hotel. There, we checked in. Again, it was a strange sensation; for weeks, we had been outdoors. Now, as I stepped into the hotel room, everything felt different. Throwing my bag on the floor, I sat on the edge of the bed, completely drained and exhausted.

The first order of business was a shower. I had dreamt of this moment from early on in the expedition. As I stripped my clothing off, I gagged at the odor of my clothing and body. I had worn the same underwear and long johns 24 hours a day since the beginning of the climb three weeks earlier. My clothing reeked. My unbathed naked body looked thin and ghastly white. It was another strange sensation as I stepped into the hot shower. I felt an incredible comfort as I let the hot water run over my head and body. It was good to get warm and clean.

I met Meegan and Ellen in the restaurant for dinner. The cold beer tasted great. I took a few sips, and then stepped into the phone booth to call home. I didn't even think about the time difference and realized that it would be late evening back in Florida. Still, I needed to let everyone there know that I was alright. My wife answered the phone, and I told her I was back at the hotel, safe and sound. She told me that she knew that we had made it to the summit and that an accident had occurred on the descent, and she was aware that someone from our group had died. She was extremely relieved to hear my voice, and promised to call friends and family to let them know that I was fine. I asked about my children and she told me they were worried about me, but were all well. My youngest daughter was away on a church mission trip and I assumed she knew nothing about our adventure. I felt better having spoken with the folks at home, knowing that they were thankful to learn that I was fine.

Back at the restaurant, I joined Ellen and Meegan at the bar. We all mentioned how wonderful our showers were, and studied the menu. I was salivating with delight; every item looked scrumptious. I ordered a burger and fries, and, after devouring that in record time, ordered chocolate cake for desert. My companions laughed at my appetite, but they ate well too. After finishing, we returned to our rooms for the evening. Climbing into a warm bed was another very unusual feeling, as I hadn't slept in a bed for three weeks. Although it was not very late, I turned off the television and lights and fell into a deep sleep.

Peace and rest at length have come,
All the day's long toil is past;
And each heart is whispering, "Home,
Home at last!"

Thomas Hood - *Home At Last*

June 12-Home at Last

After a restful sleep, I met my companions for breakfast. Meegan told us that she had not heard from Mike, meaning that the rest of our group was still weathered-in at the Denali Base Camp. Meegan and Ellen were going to stay and wait for the others. I elected to go home.

Before leaving the Base Camp, knowing that I had to return for work, Phil told me that I should feel free to leave once I got back to Talkeetna. Phil said that he would ship me any of my gear left in the group duffel bags. After breakfast, I called the transport service for a ride to the Anchorage airport.

It felt very strange to bid the others farewell. I hugged each of them, gave them my best wishes for a safe return home, and hopped into the van. Soon, I was on the long road to Anchorage.

The ride across the broad expanse of the Alaskan countryside was soothing. Although there were others in the van, I kept to myself and enjoyed the quietude. After many days of strenuous mental and physical activity, it felt good to do nothing. I turned back to look for Denali, but the grey skies hid it from my view. I wondered if Phil and the others had gotten off the mountain.

At the airport, I went to the ticket counter to find a flight home. To my chagrin, there were flights to Orlando, but they were fully booked. I arranged to fly stand-by, and hunkered down in the waiting area. It was a long wait. Again, I grew anxious and fell into a state of despair. Several flights left without me. Finally, after many hours had passed, they called my name.

The lady at the counter told me that she had a seat available for me on the next flight. Excitedly, I strode up the platform. The stewardess on board pointed me to my seat. "First class," I said in disbelief. Finally, after waiting so long to fly out of here, my luck had taken a turn for the better.

A young girl, probably 10 years old, sat in the seat next to me. "Are we in the right place?" she asked. I told her I wasn't sure, but this is where they told us to sit. She smiled up at me, apparently mature enough to appreciate our good fortune. After settling in and looking forward to the most comfortable flight of my life, a stewardess approached and told the girl and me that we were seated there in error, and she asked us to step off the plane. At first, I protested, but realized that was fruitless. I was heartbroken. The young lady and I hiked back into the terminal. After complaining to the clerk at the counter, they found seats for us in the back of the coach section. Oh well, at least I was on an airplane heading for home.

I dozed off and on as we worked our way homeward. We touched down in Minneapolis, our scheduled first stop, and I went through the same process there--waiting not so patiently for the next flight to Orlando. Finally, I boarded my airplane and was underway. Again, I slept fitfully and without great comfort for the better part of the voyage, and was glad to hear when the pilot announced that we were making the approach to Orlando. It was about 9:00 p.m., and completely dark outside. After a month without total darkness, this too, was a strange sensation. As we landed, I said a silent prayer of thanks for my safe arrival. I wanted nothing more than to reunite with my family and return to the peace and quiet of home.

Unfortunately, it was not to be. As I stepped out of the tram into the Orlando airport terminal, I was met by a bank of reporters, the bright lights of the cameras nearly blinding me. I couldn't imagine what was going on. *Why were all of these people here?*

In rapid succession, the swarm of reporters fired questions at me. Realizing that I was the center of their attention, I did my best to answer them, but quite frankly, I was in a fog. I looked around and noticed my wife, my daughter, Nicole, and several other family members, some holding "Welcome Home" signs. I was confused. Why were all of these reporters here? The frenzy lasted a few minutes, and then the members of the press suddenly departed. Finally, I was reunited with my family.

I was very happy to see my daughter, Nicole there. She has always been intelligent, mature and loaded with common sense. Amid the confusion and hubbub at the airport, she was a reassuring voice of reason, and it was very comforting to have her there. I missed my children very badly, and couldn't wait to unite with all of them. Slowly, we worked our way out of the airport and into the car, and, at long last, home.

> *It is not the critic who counts; not the man who points out where the strong man stumbled or where the doer of deeds could have done them better. The credit belongs to the man who is actually in the arena, whose face is marred with dust and sweat and blood. At best, he knows the triumph of high achievement; if he fails, at least he fails while daring greatly, so that his place shall never be with those cold and timid souls who knew neither victory or defeat.*

> Theodore Roosevelt

Return to the Real World

My fingertips are numb as I drum them on my wooden desk. Across from me, piled high, are stacks of files. Most of them contain pressing matters that need my immediate attention.

But my attention is not on those files. It is focused on my fingertips. It is a strange sensation, every finger on both hands numb only at the tips. The rest of my hands feel fine. I wonder when the sensation will return. I wonder what will happen if it doesn't.

I am suffering from frostnip, which is an initial stage of frostbite. Frostbite is dangerous and can become serious and debilitating. In cases of frostnip, the skin turns either white or red, as it did in my case, and becomes very cold. Prickling and numbness follow with continued exposure to the cold. The numbness in my fingertips started a day or so after the accident on Denali, but, being otherwise occupied, I paid no attention to it and did not notice the numbness until after I started for home.

Physically, I fared fairly well. After a few weeks at home, the frostnip in my fingertips subsided and I had numb fingertips no longer. I lost about ten pounds during the expedition. Even though I ate plenty, I burned many more calories than I consumed. My shoulder was still sore from my fall, but that, too, soon healed. The nail on one of my big toes had turned black. "Black toe" is a common problem for climbers, caused by the toe nails bumping up against the front of the boots while descending. This, too, cleared up after several weeks, although my nail is still, after all of these years, slightly deformed. Finally, I had an inguinal hernia that had to be surgically repaired.

I realized that our expedition had generated significant publicity when I met the reporters who had greeted me at the Orlando airport. Frankly, I was shocked as I had no idea that our adventure had garnered so much exposure. The first local newspaper article about our expedition appeared in the "Orlando Sentinel" on May 31. Focusing on the project Mike's middle school students were involved in, the article began: "A local man is part of an expedition to reach the summit of deadly Mt. McKinley, and the climbers' lone lifeline to the outside world is a bunch of Colorado sixth-graders who are posting news of the party's progress on the Internet." From there, interest in our expedition grew exponentially, and it was soon being followed by other newspapers and media outlets. "Climbers 'all right' in bid to conquer Mount McKinley," "Climbers make it to peak of McKinley," "McKinley climbers stranded," are samples of some of the headlines. The articles contained facts about us, the mountain, and our expedition, together with a bit of conjecture and speculation about what was going on. Aside from numerous newspaper articles, our journey was the focus of television and radio reports.

After I returned home, I received hundreds of letters, postcards and telephone calls from family members, friends, clients, even complete strangers. The large majority were supportive and congratulatory, although one or two were offensive, to say the least. One of those, sent anonymously, advised that the writer wished that I had died on the climb. On a more positive note, a humorous card from one of my clients, a middle-aged man like me, said "Why don't you take up golf like the rest of us?" The members of my church had set up a prayer chain to pray for my safe return, and I assured them that their prayers were welcome and apparently very successful.

I received many invitations to talk about the expedition, and one of the things I most enjoyed was going to local schools and speaking to students about my adventures. The younger students, in particular, loved asking questions and looking over my climbing equipment; the ice axe and crampons were foreign to the youngsters, and they were, and still are, fascinated by them.

For years afterward, I was a reluctant celebrity. I was besieged by calls from the press, family members, friends, even people I didn't know. I was often interviewed by reporters and received numerous requests to speak at events. It was slightly embarrassing for me, as I felt that I had my personal reasons for going to Denali, and I certainly didn't do it for public attention. However, I never passed up an occasion to speak, and went to every Kiwanis Club, Rotary Club, church, school or other function to tell the story of our expedition. Likewise, I never turned down an invitation to talk with the press. And I would have to say that I was treated very well by the representatives of the news media.

Often when in public, complete strangers still approach me. "You're that guy on the mountain," or "You're that mountain climber," they will say. I always try to say hello, and to speak a bit with those folks. Although my "celebrity status" has faded over time, people still remember me as the guy who climbed Mt. McKinley.

Much has happened since my trip to Denali. I continued to practice law, focusing on family law, and became certified as a family law mediator. I enjoyed mediating and helping to resolve family disputes, and that became the focus of my professional career.

After about twenty years of practicing law, I decided that I wanted to become a judge. I live in Lake County, which is part of a five-county judicial circuit.

When an opening came available for a circuit judge, I applied.

Although county and circuit judges are elected in Florida, if an opening occurs before an election is pending, the Governor fills the vacancy through an appointment process. I applied twice without success, both for positions in our circuit but outside of Lake County. I had better luck on my third attempt. A circuit judge in Lake County retired during his term, so I applied for that position. I was fortunate enough to make it through the committee process. One evening, I received a telephone call from then Governor Jeb Bush. At first, I thought it was a friend of mine trying to trick me, but it was really the Governor, and he told me that he was appointing me to the bench.

I have happily served as a circuit judge since 2002. I love the job, as it is challenging and interesting, and hope that I can hang onto it until I retire.

Since my Denali expedition, I have gotten divorced and remarried. The divorce was emotionally painful and difficult, not only for my former wife and me, but for my three grown children as well, and I hate that they had to go through that difficult process. I have much respect for my former wife. She is always an incredible mother, and I continue to have at least a civil relationship with her. Luckily, I have a tremendously close relationship with all of my children, and without them being there for me, I don't know what I would have done. Todd, Nicole and Kara, and now my three grandchildren and one great-grandchild, continue to be the center of my universe. On a recent Father's Day get-together, I looked at the three of my children as we ate breakfast together and realized how lucky I am to have them in my life. They are all great children, and, if I measure my success in life by the love we share rather than by the mountains that I have climbed, then I have truly reached a remarkable summit.

Meeting Nancy, my present wife, changed my life. She is the kindest, most decent and loving person I have ever met. She and I are active, and we enjoy many of the same interests. She is supportive and encourages me, and I have a genuine happiness that makes everything in life seem sweeter. We have now been married for a few years, and look forward to enjoying our retirement time together. She was the inspiration for writing this story; my muse in its truest sense.

I cannot downplay the impact my participation in this expedition had on my family. Obviously, they were concerned about my safety, and worried that I would be injured or killed. They were excited to be following along on our journey on the Internet, but things became more difficult when the stream of information dried up. After not hearing from us when we lost contact with Mike's students, the climbers' families developed a "support group," and they shared the news they were able to gather by e-mail and over the telephone. Dennis, with some first-hand knowledge and experience, became the guy they went to with questions, and he helped alleviate some of their concerns. The parents of the climbers, mine included, became actively involved in the chain of communication. Any bit of data was quickly disbursed throughout the group, and I know that it was comforting for my parents and family to be kept in the loop.

My youngest daughter, Kara, was in Jamaica on a church mission trip with a group of young people while I was on Denali. They were working with children in a rural hospital. While there, they had limited contact with the folks back home. Unfortunately, all that she knew was that there was an accident on Denali, and one of the members of our party was injured or killed. She did not know who it was. Obviously, this was horribly distressing to her. A few days after that, they returned to the United States, and she learned that I was fine. It had to have been very difficult for her to have gone through that stressful time, and I wish that she hadn't.

It is hard to describe to others what happens or what we go through when mountaineering. Although my family knew that it is a dangerous avocation, when it became personal, when it was their own son, brother, husband or father who was in dire circumstances, the emotional stress became real and it was overwhelming. I wish I could have summited the mountain and returned home without the deadly incident, and hate the fact that my family members had to suffer through the distress that they did.

I was lucky to have reached the summit of Denali that year. The success rate for climbers on the mountain in 1998 was a dismal 36%, much lower than the average rate of about 50%. It was the lowest rate of success in the last ten years prior to 1998. It was an El Nino season, and the bad weather was probably the culprit. The weather in May, when we started our expedition, was described as some of the worst ever experienced on Denali. The snowfall was incessant, and continuous winds, gusting to 50-80 miles per hour, were relentless at higher elevations. "It was grim," said veteran lead climbing ranger Daryl Miller. In June, the weather improved thanks to a stalled high-pressure system.

I often think about the amazing individuals I encountered during the trip to Denali. Annie Duquette has retired as Base Camp Manager on Mt. McKinley. I am sure that Denali will not be the same without her.

Ed Hommer, the climber who had prosthetic devices on both legs, did not reach the summit of Denali that year, but he did the next. After his successful ascent of Denali in 1999, Hommer wrote a book, "The Hill," which chronicled his incredible life. He did not stop climbing mountains after Denali, continuing his adventures in Alaska and the Himalayas. His attempt to be the first double amputee to summit Mt. Everest fell short when his team had to turn back because of bad weather 3,000 feet below the summit. Hommer planned to return to Everest, and went on a training trip to Mt. Rainier, which was led by Jim Wickwire. There, at a point called "Disappointment Cleaver," Ed Hommer was struck by a basketball sized rock that had fallen, and was killed instantly.

I wrote to Phil Ershler soon after we returned home from our expedition. I explained that his finest accomplishment was not getting us to the top of Denali, but in leading our broken bodies and souls down safely after we lost Chris. Phil continues to lead mountaineering expeditions around the world. When they reached the summit of Mt. Everest in 2002, Phil and his wife, Susan, became the first couple to climb the seven summits, the highest peak on each of the seven continents. The Ershlers are sought-after motivational speakers.

Mike and Meegan got married shortly after our expedition. Kara, my former wife and I had the pleasure of attending their beautiful wedding in Vail Pass, Colorado. Sadly, however, I lost contact with those amazing individuals I climbed with. Mike, Meegan, Dennis, Romulo and Ellen were all remarkable people, and I was lucky to have had the opportunity to get to know them. Although we were together a relatively short period of time, we were intimately thrust together in circumstances in which all emotions were intensified. Particularly with Mike and Meegan since I had spent so much time with them, we laughed and cried together, and we depended upon each other as if connected by some invisible life support system. I wish I had done a better job of staying in contact with all of them after we returned home, and I often wonder what happened to them and how they are. I have no explanation for why I didn't stay in touch, and take the blame for my failure to do so. Maybe that was my way to avoid bubbling up the bad taste of Chris's death.

I gave up mountaineering. Right after my trip to Denali, a fellow climbing buddy, another "weekend warrior," wisely advised me to do another easier climb, just to show that I could. I wish I had followed his advice. I think it may have boosted my confidence, but maybe it would have been foolish. In any event, I didn't follow his guidance.

To be truthful, I still felt a lingering fear of alpine climbing. Following my McKinley trip, on a visit to Grandfather Mountain in North Carolina with my daughters, I embarrassed myself when I froze in fear when the wind blew while we were crossing a small bridge between two rocky peaks near the top of the mountain. They and other tourists walked across it very easily, while I stood immobilized with a death grip on each hand rail. The wind, it seemed, forced unspeakable memories to surface.

After the Denali expedition, I did plenty of hiking in the mountains of north Georgia and North Carolina, often going with my daughter, Kara, as her teaching schedule permitted her to take time off to do that with me. I truly enjoyed our time together, and it reminded me of when we participated in the YMCA Indian Princess program when she was a child. Once, when my former wife and I traveled to visit her family in Las Vegas, Kara, who was still a high school student, came along, and she and I took a side trip to climb Mt. Whitney. We signed on with a guide and took a different route than the standard one to the summit. Unfortunately, Kara had just recovered from the flu and was feeling miserable when we got higher up, so we turned around and descended. Despite that, we still enjoyed camping and hiking in the beautiful high Sierra Mountains of California.

While hiking with Kara on Mt. Whitney, I was often worried about her. Once, particularly, when we were crossing a cliff face on a narrow trail, I was quietly troubled as we slowly inched across. Concerned that Kara could fall, I reached my hand toward her backpack, hoping that I might grab her if she did. This was the first time on a climb that I was really concerned and worried about someone other than myself, someone so close to me, and it truly added a new dynamic to the experience.

I often thought about Willi Unsoeld and the death of his daughter. Unsoeld was a famous American mountaineer. As part of the first American team to summit Mt. Everest in 1963, he and another climber split off from the main group and summited the mountain by the difficult West Ridge route. Unsoeld lost nine of his toes to frostbite and spent several months in the hospital recovering. He lived in Washington, where he became a leader in outdoor education. Willi Unsoeld climbed Mt. Rainier over 200 times.

Willi had a daughter, and he named her after the beautiful Himalayan mountain, Nanda Devi, the second highest peak in India. Nanda Devi is a very difficult mountain to climb, and in 1976 Willi led an expedition there. One of the members of his team was his daughter, Nanda Devi. There, Willi's idea of spiritual growth through mortal risk would be dreadfully challenged.

Nanda developed a stomach illness during the expedition. After spending several days climbing at high altitudes, she became very ill. She said "I am going to die," then passed into unconsciousness. Despite their diligent efforts to revive her, the party was unable to do so and she died. I can only imagine the pain and grief that Willi suffered. Having shared the joy of the mountaineering experience with his daughter, he then had to suffer the lonely pain of her demise. After that, Willi continued to climb, but unfortunately lost his life when he was captured in an avalanche while leading a group of college students on a climb of Mt. Rainier in 1979.

When she had graduated from college, I had told Kara that I would take her to Africa, a promise I had failed to fulfill. Years later, after I was divorced, I decided to go. I invited all of my children, but Todd and Nicole could not go. Kara, who was teaching and available to go over the summer, was able to join me.

We signed up for a two week trip to Tanzania. The first week included a climb of Mount Kilimanjaro, the highest mountain in Africa at 19,318 feet, while the second week consisted of a wildlife photo safari. The trip to Africa was incredible, and, along with Denali, was the adventure of a lifetime for me. The climb of Kilimanjaro was a difficult hike through some of the most amazing landscapes on earth. We witnessed remarkable examples of flora and fauna, while being led up the mountain by interesting local guides. We also had the opportunity to trek together with fascinating and friendly people. When we arrived at the high camp, Kara had developed a nasty cough, and I wasn't feeling well at all, so we opted out of the summit bid, and descended with one of the guides the next day. Despite having failed to reach the summit, we have unforgettably good memories of our time on the mountain.

Our safari the following week was just as mesmerizing. We were driven by our guide to Lake Manyara and Segengeti National Parks, where we saw every kind of African wildlife imaginable. We visited the Olduvai Gorge in the Great Rift Valley where the earliest human fossils were found. We saw the Ngorongoro Crater, and then went on to the Tangire National Park. We finished our tour with a visit to a Masai tribe, which was an incredible and unforgettable experience.

Africa is truly a remarkable and unique place, and the people are exceptional. I will never forget our time there, and it was one of the most extraordinary experiences of my life.

If you have built castles in the air, your work need not be lost; that is where they should be. Now put the foundations under them.

Henry David Thoreau – *Walden*

Climbing Again?

I stood on the Muir snowfield looking up. The weather was pleasant, almost warm. Ahead, up and beyond my sight, stood Camp Muir, our destination for the day, and much further beyond, the summit of Mt. Rainier. Feeling energetic, I smiled and marched on.

Nearly ten years after I had climbed Denali, my last alpine expedition, and despite having vowed never to do this again, I returned to Mt. Rainier. A couple of prosecutors who worked at the courthouse convinced me to go along with them. I worked out, trained, and prepared for the trip, but I was worried that I was not fit enough to do it, nor mentally ready for the challenge of another high alpine climb.

As I ascended the snowfield, I felt strong and climbed well. I had more alpine climbing experience than the assistant guides who accompanied us, and I felt confident and emotionally sound. Without much difficulty, I climbed with our team to the high camp. However, when we bedded down for the night prior to the early morning summit attempt, I had a headache and could not sleep well. Although I have felt like this on expeditions before, and continued climbing when I did, I rolled up in my sleeping bag and imagined that horrible things would happen. The wind rattled my tent, which rattled my brain. I lost all confidence, and willed myself to feel worse than I did. I talked myself out of a summit bid, rationalizing that I have been to the summit of Rainier twice before, and didn't need to risk attempting to go there again. Really, like we used to say as kids, I "chickened out."

Around midnight, as the others awoke and prepared for the climb to the summit, feeling embarrassed, I told our guide that I didn't feel well and would stay behind. My tent mate, Mike, clambered out to join the other climbers. Among the excited voices, I heard the other prosecutor, John. Unfortunately, I would not join them.

After my experiences on Kilimanjaro and Rainier, I wondered about my ability to climb above 14,000 feet. One summer, on a family trip to Breckenridge, I decided to attempt a climb of Mt. Elbert, the highest peak in Colorado. At 14,440 feet in altitude, it is the highest mountain in the Rockies and, after Mt. Whitney, the second highest peak in the contiguous United States.

Besides seeing if I could hike above 14,000 feet, I had another motive for climbing Elbert. Over the years, I have been lucky enough to have reached the peaks of the highest points in several states: Alaska (Denali), Georgia (Brasstown Bald), Hawaii (Mauna Kea), New Hampshire (Mt. Washington), North Carolina (Mt. Mitchell), Tennessee (Clingman's Dome) and

Washington (Mt. Rainier). Although I harbored no ambitions of becoming a "Highpointer," someone who reaches the highest peak in each of the fifty states, I thought that it might be nice to add Colorado to my list.

A climb of Mt. Elbert in the summer is basically a long uphill hike. There is usually no snow, and the trail is well marked. Most of the hike is above the tree line. Although strenuous, the climb is not technically difficult, but violent afternoon thunderstorms and lightening are dangerous. For this reason, I did as most other hikers do, and began climbing very early in the morning so as to be off the mountain by early afternoon.

Although I felt nauseous at one point, I made it to the summit without incident. It felt great to be there, and, together with several other climbers, I enjoyed the tremendous views overlooking the rocky peaks and lush valleys of the mountain range. I was very happy that I was able to make it to that altitude, and felt as if I made a wise choice in climbing Mt. Elbert.

And now we get down to two magic words that tell us how to accomplish just about anything we want to accomplish, two powerful words that can change any situation, two dynamic words that all too few people use. And what are these two amazing words? Do it!

Norman Vincent Peale - *Power of the Plus Factor*

Denali's Lasting Impression

Not many days pass that I don't think about Chris Hooyman. His body was recovered on June 13, one week after his fatal fall. By then, the weather had cleared enough that the National Park Service was able to locate and retrieve his body, which was found nearly 1,000 feet below the ridge he had plummeted from.

I communicated with Chris's mother, Nancy Hooyman, soon after my return from Denali. To say the least, it was very difficult. I know that Chris was dearly loved by his family and friends, and they were obviously having a challenging time coming to grips with his death. In a letter to Nancy, I carefully described my recollection of the events surrounding his fall, and she wrote back, explaining that it had helped her to better understand what had occurred.

In the days following my homecoming, I learned much more about Chris Hooyman. I discovered that he was an amazing individual, well-liked by many, and that he had a positive impact on the lives of many others. He was a kind, sensitive man who loved the outdoors.

Having had ample time to reflect on why Chris did what he did on Denali, I think I know the answer. Aware that I was in trouble, Chris reacted instinctively. Without considering the consequences to himself, he went to render assistance. It is noteworthy that Mike Vanderbeek, the volunteer ranger who went to the aid of a climber on Denali, died in the same manner in nearly the same spot as Chris did. By jumping into action to save a fallen climber, Vanderbeek likely did the same thing that Chris did; he acted instinctively without considering his own safety. Their actions remind me of those heroic firefighters, police officers and emergency personnel who ran into the burning and crumbling World Trade Center on that fateful day in New York City. Whether their decisions were right or wrong, wise or unwise, carefully considered or not, their actions are driven by a good-hearted desire to aid their fellow man. They are far better people than I am.

In all the years that have passed since my Denali trip, I have never lost the urge to climb. It is in my blood. There is something indescribably good in standing on the side of a big mountain, breathing in the fresh, crisp air, a brilliant sun burning in a cold cobalt-blue sky, hooked by rope to other similar-minded beings, while looking up toward a distant, hidden goal. There is also a certain glory in knowing that you are different, not better, just different from those individuals who don't willingly subject themselves to the dangers and the highs and lows of climbing big mountains, those who do not welcome the isolation from the real world or embrace the discomfort of living in the same clothes in cold, uncomfortable tents. It is a test of will, of the force of common sense over desire, to stay away from those mountains.

Hundreds of times, I have been asked, "Why did you do this?", or "Why climb mountains?" Intuitively, I know the answer, but it is tough to explain.

In a response that has become famous, when asked why he attempted to climb Mt. Everest, Sir George Mallory answered: "Because it is there." Jon Krakauer, in his excellent book "Into Thin Air," addressed the issue in much more eloquent words than I. He said:

> People who don't climb mountains-- the great majority of humankind, that is to say--tend to assume that the sport is a reckless, Dionysian pursuit of ever escalating thrills. But the notion that climbers are merely adrenaline junkies chasing a righteous fix is a fallacy, at least in the case of Everest. What I was doing up there had almost nothing in common with bungee jumping or skydiving or riding a motorcycle at 120 miles per hour.
>
> ...I'd always known that climbing mountains was a high-risk pursuit. I accepted that danger was an essential component of the game--without it, climbing would be little different from a

hundred other trifling diversions. It was titillating to brush up against the enigma of mortality, to steal a glimpse across its forbidden frontier. Climbing was a magnificent activity, I firmly believed, not in spite of the inherent perils, but precisely because of them.

Whatever the motivation, there is something special about mountaineering, and there is no question that my life is much richer and fuller because I climbed.

Undoubtedly, my experiences on Denali had a major impact on my life. Those experiences, both good and bad, have helped shape the person that I became, and are woven into the fabric of my being. I have always had an optimistic attitude, and believe that my experiences on Denali strengthened my positive outlook toward all things in life. As anyone who climbs mountains will tell you, soon after finishing a climb, one forgets the bad things and remembers the good. Perhaps that is what keeps us going back. That was far more difficult after my experiences on Denali, but I have learned that that adage is true of just about everything in life. In truth, since my McKinley expedition, everything in life has been easier for me to deal with. Frankly, I have probably done the hardest thing I will ever do in life.

Likewise, I have always been goal oriented, but after Denali, I became more focused about my aspirations, and I worked diligently and passionately toward accomplishing them. I have worked intensely all of my life, and after Denali, I have come to a better understanding of how hard work produces good results. I have always believed that we are the masters of our own destinies, but after Denali, I know with certainty that that is true.

Although I was a patient person before McKinley, I now know the real meaning of patience. Good things in life have come to me because I waited for them, knowing that they would come.

My expedition to Denali reinforced for me the notion that each of us is responsible for taking care of ourselves. I have stayed in good physical condition, and now, together with my wife, I ride bikes, hike, ski and exercise regularly. I try my best, sometimes unsuccessfully, to eat properly.

Certainly the experience taught me to put things in better perspective. I discovered a settled peacefulness that I did not have before.

I learned that it is not necessarily the places we visit, but more importantly the people we are with when we visit them. Although Denali is an incredibly beautiful visual feast, I would not have wanted to enjoy it with anyone other than the wonderful people who were there with me. Upon my return home from Denali, I experienced the caring love of the people around me, and I learned how much we really matter to each other. Thus, I acquired a better appreciation for people, and my fondness for the mountains will never surpass the love I have for my family and friends.

One of the most important lessons I have learned from my climbing experience is that it is good to dream big dreams. I was an average guy who did something extraordinary in life. I never would have reached the top of the mountain had I not dreamed to do so.

I also learned a lesson about Yin and Yang. According to Chinese philosophy, Yin and Yang describe the order in the natural world in which opposite forces interact and are interdependent. While conflicting, these forces are equal and complementary. Many dualities, such as fire and water, light and dark, good and evil, are considered manifestations of the conflicting dual forces symbolized by Yin and Yang.

Hot and cold, happiness and sadness, pleasure and pain; this is the story of the Yin and Yang of Denali, as it is the Yin and Yang of life.

Perhaps, when people ask me why I climbed mountains, I can honestly say that those are the reasons. I know for certain that my life is infinitely richer for the experience I had on Denali, and I can truly say that it has been an epic adventure.

Bibliography

These are some books about Denali and mountaineering that I have enjoyed:

Bass, Dick, and Frank Wells with Rick Ridgeway, *Seven Summits,* New York: Warner Books, 1986.

Brill, David, *Desire and Ice: Searching for Perspective Atop Denali.* Washington, D.C.: 2002.

Coombs, Colby, *Denali's West Buttress: A Climber's Guide to Mount McKinley's Classic Route.* Seattle: The Mountaineers, 1997.

Davidson, Art, *Minus 148: First Winter Ascent of Mt. McKinley.* Seattle: The Mountaineers, 1999.

Eng, Ronald, ed., *Mountaineering: The Freedom of the Hills*, 8th edition. Seattle: The Mountaineers, 2010.

Ershler, Phil and Susan, *Together on Top of the World: The Remarkable Story of the First Couple to Climb the Fabled Seven Summits.* New York: Warner Books, 2007.

Horrell, Mark, *Denali Nights: A Commercial Expedition to Climb Mt. McKinley's West Buttress,* Mountain Footsteps Press, 2014.

Krakauer, Jon, *Into Thin Air: A Personal Account of the Mt. Everest Disaster,* New York: Villard Books, 1997.

Roskelley, John, *Nanda Devi: The Tragic Expedition,* Seattle: Mountaineers Books, 2000.

Washburn, Bradford, and David Roberts, *Mount McKinley: The Conquest of Denali.* New York: Abradale Press, 2000.

Waterman, Jonathan, *In the Shadow of Denali: Life and Death on Alaska's Mt. McKinely.* New York: Lyons Press, 2009.

Wickwire, Jim, and Dorothy Bullitt, *Addicted to Danger: A Memoir about Affirming Life in the Face of Death.* New York: Pocket Books, 1998.

Acknowledgements

Thank you to my parents, Joan and Jim, who have always been supportive and are the inspiration for every goal that I have accomplished.

Thank you to my children Todd, Nicole, and Kara, and their spouses or significant others, Karen, Michael and Jordan, and my grandchildren, Kimberly, Blake and Cecelia, who have all made me proud beyond my dreams and have shown me the true meaning of unconditional love.

Thank you to my wife, Nancy, for encouraging me to reach for the stars, and for loving me and providing me unbelievable happiness.

Thank you to my brothers and sister, for being good siblings and friends. And thank you to my sister, Judy, who watches over us and is always with us in spirit, and who is surely very proud of the family we have become.

Thank you to those good people who read and edited drafts of this book, especially to Dotty Carrier, Kirsten McLain, and Kara Hymel.

Thank you to Phil Ershler, for guiding me safely to the tops of mountains, and for showing me that climbing mountains is more than a sport.

Thank you to Dennis, Mike, Meegan, Romelo, and Ellen, for being integral parts of my adventure on Denali. And thank you to Chris Hooyman, for your inspiring life.

About the Author

Larry Semento is a Circuit Judge in Tavares, Florida. Born in New Jersey, his family moved to South Carolina after he graduated from high school. Larry has a Bachelor of Arts degree from the University of South Carolina, and a Juris Doctor degree from the University of Florida College of Law. He practiced law in Eustis, Florida for twenty years before being appointed as a Circuit Court Judge. Larry has been a judge for twelve years and has handled criminal, civil, and family law cases during his tenure.

Many of the legal commentaries Larry has written have been published, including a recent law review article. This is his first non-legal publication.

Larry lives in Eustis, Florida with his wife, Nancy. He has three children, three grandchildren and one great-grandchild. He enjoys hiking, biking, and many other outdoor activities.

Thank You

Thank you for reading my story. I hope that you enjoyed it. Please write a review of the book on my page on Amazon.com; that would be very helpful. Thanks!

Made in the USA
San Bernardino, CA
02 May 2017